Management Extra

DEVELOPMENT FOR
HIGH PERFORMANCE

Development Continuum Ltd
Learning and Development

15 Timber Court, Hillmorton Road
RUGBY, Warks, CV22 5AZ

Tel: 01788 547975 Mobile: 07921 815551

Management Extra

DEVELOPMENT FOR HIGH PERFORMANCE

Routledge
Taylor & Francis Group
New York   London

First Published by Elsevier

This edition published 2011 by Routledge
2 Park Square, Milton Park, Abingdon, Oxon, OX14 4RN
711 Third Avenue, New York, NY 10017, USA
Routledge is an imprint of Taylor & Francis Group, an Informa business.

First published 2005
Revised edition 2008

Notice
No responsibility is assumed by the publisher for any injury and/or damage
to persons or property as a matter of products liability, negligence or
otherwise, or from any use or operation of any methods, products,
instructions or ideas contained in the material herein.

British Library Cataloguing in Publication Data
A catalogue record for this book is available from the British Library

Library of Congress Cataloging-in-Publication Data
A catalog record for this book is available from the Library of Congress

ISBN 978-0-08-055480-8

Transferred to Digital Printing 2010

Contents

Activities

Figures

Tables

Series preface

Whether you are a tutor/trainer or studying management development to further your career, Management Extra provides an exciting and flexible resource helping you to achieve your goals. The series is completely new and up-to-date, and has been written to harmonise with the 2004 national occupational standards in management and leadership. It has also been mapped to management qualifications, including the Institute of Leadership & Management's middle and senior management qualifications at Levels 5 and 7 respectively on the revised national framework.

For learners, coping with all the pressures of today's world, Management Extra offers you the flexibility to study at your own pace to fit around your professional and other commitments. Suddenly, you don't need a PC or to attend classes at a specific time – choose when and where to study to suit yourself! And, you will always have the complete workbook as a quick reference just when you need it.

For tutors/trainers, Management Extra provides an invaluable guide to what needs to be covered, and in what depth. It also allows learners who miss occasional sessions to 'catch up' by dipping into the series.

This series provides unrivalled support for all those involved in management development at middle and senior levels.

Reviews of Management Extra

I have utilised the Management Extra series for a number of Institute of Leadership and Management (ILM) Diploma in Management programmes. The series provides course tutors with the flexibility to run programmes in a variety of formats, from fully facilitated, using a choice of the titles as supporting information, to a tutorial based programme, where the complete series is provided for home study. These options also give course participants the flexibility to study in a manner which suits their personal circumstances. The content is interesting, thought provoking and up-to-date, and, as such, I would highly recommend the use of this series to suit a variety of individual and business needs.

Martin Davies BSc(Hons) MEd CEngMIMechE MCIPD FITOL FInstLM
Senior Lecturer, University of Wolverhampton Business School

At last, the complete set of books that make it all so clear and easy to follow for tutor and student. A must for all those taking middle/senior management training seriously.

Michael Crothers, ILM National Manager

Helping your team become high performers

Teams don't become high performers by accident – it takes training, development and time to turn an average team into a high performing one.

Your role

Teams need to be coached and trained, so that they develop skills and learn to work together effectively. Team members can learn from each other, as well as from training programmes. Your role in this is vital. By identifying appropriate developmental activities, you can help your team go from good to great!

As the team leader, you also need to look at your own behaviour. You need to examine the way you handle problems with performance, and the way that you give your team the feedback that they need to learn. And you need to assess the development process, so that your team becomes even more effective over time.

Your objectives are to:

- Identify how employee development is linked to organisational performance
- Develop employees by leading, coaching, mentoring and delegating
- Identify opportunities for people development when faced with organisational changes
- Explore the competency framework and use it to highlight individual and team development needs
- Apply the key steps within a performance management process
- Evaluate the effectiveness of training and development activities.

1 Development and improved performance

In an effective organisation, there should be an alignment of goals and objectives. Everyone's effort should be aligned so that every part of the organisation is working together and pulling in the same direction.

As a manager you are at the hub of your organisation – with a close understanding of the needs of your team, together with a strategic understanding of the needs of your business. This gives you a central role as a developer in the organisation. This theme asks you to consider the development process and use the development cycle to help you frame development activities for your team.

In this theme you will:

◆ **Examine the links between employee development and the organisation's goals**

◆ **Identify your role as a manager in developing individuals**

◆ **Explore the steps involved in the individual, team and organisational development process.**

Linking development and organisational performance

A key feature of the role of managers is to safeguard and develop the resources that they have been given. They are often supported in this role by the training and development (T&D) department or the human resources (HR) department. Such departments have a responsibility to help standardise and align training and development practices across the whole organisation.

In a business climate where new products and services, increased customer expectations and competition are the norm, organisations are increasingly dependent on having competent staff. The key resource in organisations is now knowledge and what has become known as intellectual capital. Skill and expertise in applying that knowledge is still the key differentiator between competing organisations. Investment in staff development must therefore be linked clearly to the overall aims, strategies and business plans of the organisation.

People – a key resource

> **Not everything that can be counted counts, and not everything that counts can be counted.**
>
> **Albert Einstein**
> **(1879–1955)**

Measuring the contribution of people to the performance of an organisation is not easy; but evidence of the link between organisational performance and people management is mounting. The nice words about people being the organisation's greatest asset may well be true, even if organisations don't always realise it in practice. Here are details of one study that supports the idea that people are very important to organisational performance.

A study by Linda Bilmes, Peter Strueven and Konrad Wetzker, of the Boston Consulting Group, sought to measure how well companies manage employees. They developed a 'people scorecard' – a set of criteria that can be tracked and quantified. The scorecard looked at HR functions such as recruiting, training and performance assessment and also what they call 'intrapreneurship' – creating an active entrepreneurial culture in the company. The study analysed more than two hundred companies in the US and Germany. Each company was rated and compared with industry peers.

The researchers found a relationship between successful companies and those companies that had effective HR and intrapreneurial activities. Companies that scored highest had a higher total shareholder return than lower-scoring companies. In the US, top companies had an average annual return of 27 per cent over the period 1989–1998, whereas the bottom ones earned 8 per cent. Companies with middle scores had an average return of 21 per cent, which is close to the 19.2 per cent average annual growth in Standard & Poor's 500 index.

In Germany, companies with the highest score had a shareholder return nearly three times higher than companies with the lowest score and 35 per cent above the median.

Bilmes suggests that companies can begin to create an emphasis on people by following eight basic steps:

- Top-level commitment
- Workforce development planning – regular assessment of business needs coupled with an assessment of how the workforce must change
- Develop versatility – use development to meet business needs, but also to build the flexibility of the workforce
- Training – linked to the personal and career development of the individual
- Retain good workers – linking compensation to performance can influence employees' loyalty

♦ Structure work to foster intrapreneurship and decentralised decision making

♦ Reward success – linking performance to compensation and reward attributes such as creativity, teamwork and skills development

♦ Communicate the people factor.

Source: *Bilmes* (2001)

This study suggests that organisations that invest in their people perform better. A key aspect of this investment is to provide for development that is aligned to the organisation's needs.

Alignment of effort

Organisations recognise the need to create close alignment between goals that are set at a corporate level and those set at a local level. The idea here is that goals are cascaded down through organisational levels. This is not an easy task and at each level ambiguity will exist and a degree of mismatch has to be accepted. However, the intention is clear in that organisational goals should be used to focus efforts throughout the organisation. It is also obvious that this process of cascading can be used to identify and initiate development and training at each level. In this way the performance that is required to meet these objectives can be achieved.

Figure 1.1 illustrates this principle of cascading and linking in an organisation by showing how the goals at each level can be used to trigger a development activity. Change becomes a regular feature of organisational life as both goals and individual competencies are never static. It is the drive for alignment that creates the excitement that surrounds the issue of staff development – the more successful organisations being those that have mastered this process.

Figure 1.1 *Alignment of effort*

Development means different things to different people. We are defining it as an event or process which helps people to learn, however the event occurs. However, in a business context, development is any event which enables an individual or team to perform better. This becomes more obvious when we look at development in the following three broad categories:

Technical/functional development

This is job-specific and is normally associated with the specialist skills or knowledge required for the performance of the role. Examples are jobs in engineering, building, computing, accounting, medicine, selling, customer service, marketing, production and manufacturing. Therefore, an individual will expect to be kept up to date and developed across a range of technical topics and skills necessary for effective execution of their job. Continual professional development is often incorporated into this area.

Personal development

This builds the underpinning skills and knowledge that each individual should possess to enable them to perform any role well. Examples are skills in communications, presentation, assertiveness, influencing and teamworking. These are often referred to as 'soft' skills and they are particular to the individual rather than to the job.

Management development

This relates to the need to manage people effectively so that the team or department meets its performance targets. The components of management development vary between organisations, but may typically include team building, performance management, objective setting and agreement, developing staff, appraisals, motivating staff, leadership, managing information, health and safety, quality, budgets, decision making, problem solving, managing risks and managing change.

Linking development to work

Organisations that deliberately create opportunities for people to learn and acquire new skills want a return on their investment. They need people to apply their newly acquired learning and skills for organisational benefit. If this does not occur, then the organisation is wasting both resources and time. Organisations invest in developing people for the following reasons:

- to help people perform better in their job
- to help prepare people for other employment within the organisation
- to retain key people within the organisation
- to build up a capability that is needed for planned changes in organisational direction.

Striking the balance between creating the type of organisation immortalised in the Charlie Chaplin film, *Modern Times*, in which people were expected to behave like machines, and one where the workplace is seen as an opportunity for total self-indulgence is the task faced by the chief executive. Managers are also charged with helping to maintain that balance once it has been struck. Look at the following case study:

The ABC organisation is heavily committed to staff development. Each year the training and development department issues its training catalogue of courses which all staff members can attend. These courses cover a wide variety of personal, technical and management development. The costs of all courses are borne by the training and development department central budget. Provided individuals have the agreement of their manager or team leader, they can attend courses. Nominations are taken in the order in which they are received. As the department normally uses its budget by the end of Quarter three, people tend to book and attend early to ensure they get onto the courses.

Symptoms in the ABC organisation which indicate that the balance has not been struck correctly are that:

- there are no direct links between the training and development activities, the organisational strategy, business plans, team objectives and individual needs
- there are no performance management and development planning processes within the organisation

- development activities and provision are not tailored to the individual businesses

- individuals see development as primarily for their personal benefit, rather than organisational needs

- departments are reluctant to give staff time for development

- the training department is driving development rather than working in conjunction with the business heads and line managers to ensure that their needs are being met.

Performance management and development

Performance management is about managing employee performance to achieve organisational objectives. A key aspect of this is probably the performance review or appraisal, but in many organisations with performance management systems, performance and development are inextricably linked. Figure 1.2 shows the four stages of a typical performance management system.

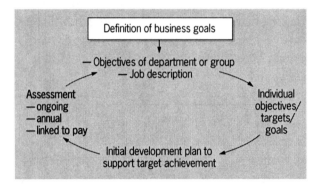

Figure 1.2 *Stages in a typical performance management system*

Source: *Torrington and Hall* (1998)

The typical process in Figure 1.2 shows that objective setting is cascaded from strategy formulation, down through the business to the individual level. These objectives support the identification of gaps in knowledge and skills and a development plan is agreed to enable individuals to meet these needs. There is ongoing assessment of progress, but this culminates in an annual performance appraisal or review. Note that in this model the appraisal is linked to pay assessment. However, this is not always the case as it can undermine some of the core benefits of the appraisal process. The most crucial aspect of this model is its close association with the development process.

Communication channels

Open and frequently used channels of communication are essential if organisations are going to succeed in aligning their performance management activities with business goals. Information must flow up, down and across the organisation so that the organisation's strategies are in tune with the organisation's on-the-ground activities. For example, information about business goals and priorities must cascade down throughout the organisation so that they can be accurately translated and converted to appropriate objectives and targets at every part and level of the business. Information about resource requirements, development needs, targets, customer requirements and employee attitudes must flow up so that senior management can keep in touch with business operations. Formal communication channels may be designed to give and collect information, and include team briefings, procedures and policy documents, newsletters, employee attitude surveys and regular reporting procedures.

Regular communication in the performance management system may include the following:

- Senior management communicates overall changes in organisational performance and changes in strategies and goals

- Agreement between managers and senior management on goals and targets at different parts and levels of the business and then on resource requirements

- Managers agree goals and targets with teams and individuals

- Managers and individual members of staff agree individual development – recorded on individual development plans

- Managers consolidate individual development plans into team/department or unit development plans and senior managers evaluate the organisation's consolidated development plan to agree priority areas which will best support organisational strategies

- Managers and individuals review individual progress and performance in annual appraisals which are consolidated and communicated to human resources and senior management

- Managers report to staff, human resources and senior management on changes in behaviour and skills resulting from development and the impact this has on performance

- Senior management reviews and communicates changes in organisational performance – some of which may be attributed to development events – and establishes new goals.

Activity 1

How do you contribute to organisational strategy?

Objective

In an effective organisation, there should be an alignment of goals and objectives. This activity will help to show how your efforts contribute to the overall organisational strategy.

Figure 1.3 *Alignment of effort*

Task

1 Think about your goals and how they relate to what higher and lower levels in your organisation are seeking to achieve. Summarise your goals in the relevant row in the chart and then write in the goals for teams and units above and below you, including the organisation's strategic goals.

You may need to do some research to fill in any gaps in your knowledge and to make sure you really know what is going on around you.

Organisational level	Summary of goals
Strategic	
Business unit	

Organisational level	Summary of goals
Department	
Individual/team leader	
Team	
Individual/team member	

2　Now identify specific objectives for yourself, your manager and your team. Are there clear links in the objectives at each level? Are your objectives aligned and contributing to the same ends?

My objectives are:

My manager's objectives are:

My team's objectives are:

Feedback

The alignment of goals and objectives ensures that everyone is pulling in the same direction to achieve the company strategy, and that the efforts of the organisation and its people are not wasted.

If you have difficulties seeing how goals and objectives at different levels of the organisation are aligned, you could discuss this with your manager, or compare your findings with your colleagues.

If people can see a clear connection between what they are doing in their work and what their organisation is seeking to achieve, they can see how their contribution helps the organisation and appreciate its importance. This can help in developing commitment. Do the members of your team know how their objectives link to both your objectives and those of your manager? How can you explain how they contribute to the organisation?

The development process

Here we explore the development process and your role as a manager within this process.

The development cycle

Theorists have described development as being part of a continuous cycle rather than a series of discrete events or activities – see Figure 1.4. In this cycle there are close links between the individual and organisational development processes. Here we assume that as the organisation changes and grows then individual capabilities must also grow. For both the individual and the organisation, the stages of needs identification, planning to satisfy the need, taking action and finally evaluating the need are followed.

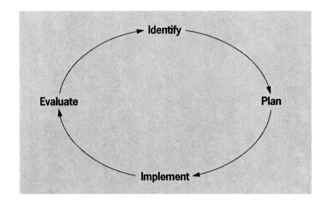

Figure 1.4 *The development cycle*

Identify

The process of identifying development needs is usually a combination of bottom-up and top-down processes. Managers at all levels must first clearly understand the organisational context for development before any other steps are taken. This means that you need to answer the following questions:

- What are the organisation's strategies for the future and what are they expected to achieve within the next one to three years? It is important, especially at middle and senior manager levels, that a longer-term view is taken.

- What are the goals that have to be achieved?

- How are they to be achieved? Are there any special factors that need to be taken into consideration?

- Are the goals new or challenging?

Having identified and understood the context for development, you need to discuss this with members of your team. Some organisations adopt a two-stage approach to these discussions:

- Stage 1: Individuals undertake their own gap analysis – to identify where they need to develop skills in order to meet their goals – and suggest development remedies, before passing the draft plan to their manager

- Stage 2: The manager reviews each plan with individuals, confirming or discussing the gap analysis, priority areas for development, options for undertaking the development, together with the timescales involved.

It is acceptable for these discussions to take place within performance reviews.

Plan

Having agreed individual needs, these are consolidated into the team, department, business and organisational development plans. This process should establish the links between individual and organisational development plans.

Planning determines how it is all going to happen. Managers have to ensure that work is being done and performance targets are being met, while enabling individuals to undertake development. Common planning areas at all levels of an organisation may include:

- the development that is going to happen, and clear links to business needs
- the priority
- who will receive development in specific areas
- when it is going to happen
- how it will happen
- booking people onto courses and programmes, job swaps, secondments, etc.
- booking venues, trainers and facilitators
- ensuring the budgets are in place
- ongoing measurement and evaluation of effectiveness of development.

Types of development activity

These can be divided into off-job and on-job activities.

Examples of **off-job development activities** – these take learners away from their work:

- training courses/programmes
- off-site residential programmes and day programmes
- computer-based training at a learning suite
- networking/formal learning groups
- reading a book.

Examples of **on-job development activities** – these are integrated into learners' work:

- job swap
- secondments
- projects
- job shadowing
- coaching
- delegation
- on-job mentoring.

Implement

Implementation is the plan in action and involves managers, training and development staff and those who are undergoing development.

It is good practice to agree the planned activities and outcomes with staff involved in any development activity. This means covering aspects such as:

- the business reason why the organisation is investing in the development activity
- what the individual is expected to contribute to the activity
- the outputs that are expected and how they will be evaluated
- how the development will be applied to work.

Review

Reviewing or evaluating the effectiveness of learning and development can be done at an individual level, as well as at the organisational level.

Many large organisations typically spend about one per cent of turnover on development activities. This investment has to be justified. Organisations are increasingly concerned about measuring the value derived from staff development. This may involve identifying all areas of development expenditure, including lost opportunity costs of people being away from the workplace, and measuring these costs against the benefits that accrue to the organisation when people apply their new learning or skills on return to work.

Reviewing the outcomes of development activities thus becomes an essential activity in the challenge of developing people for high performance.

The manager's role in development

As long ago as 1974, Peter Drucker identified the five basic operations of the manager:

- setting objectives
- organising
- motivating and encouraging
- measuring
- developing people, including oneself.

Source: *Drucker* (1974)

Developing people is a key role for managers. Development takes place in an organisational context and involves learning. As a developer, the first question to resolve is how does individual development and learning relate to the needs of the organisation itself? We can see that individuals are able to learn but the idea that organisations can also learn may require a leap of the imagination, but there are similarities. The question we ask of individuals is what they have to learn to do well. The same question can also apply to an organisation. The organisation needs to be able to:

13

- interface with the outside world in such a way that the stakeholders and customers achieve satisfaction
- be efficient and effective in conducting its internal affairs, in particular by having a structure that supports the key processes and delivers outputs to meet performance requirements
- create an environment in which people can be effective in pursuing the purpose of the enterprise.

It is not unreasonable to assume that managers at all levels are concerned with helping the enterprise learn how to achieve these three capabilities. The next level of learning is that pursued within the enterprise and involves team learning. The question here is: 'What does the group need to learn to do well?' There are four key requirements:

- to manage the interface with other internal groups
- to satisfy customers and stakeholders
- to turn hidden and personal knowledge into knowledge that can be shared
- to work together effectively as a team.

The final level of learning is the individual level. There are three basic areas of individual learning:

- mastering the local environment
- contributing to the team
- pursuing personal development and growth.

The drivers for learning at these three levels – organisational, team and individual – stem from the requirements and demands of the enterprise. They will include directives from corporate staff, from senior management and from individuals' perceptions of what is required of them. The largest tangible drivers of learning will, of course, stem from the work itself.

As a manager you are at the hub of your organisation – with a close understanding of the needs of your staff together with a strategic understanding of the needs of your business. This gives you a central role as a developer in your organisation. Figure 1.5 shows the manager operating at the hub of a network of opportunities.

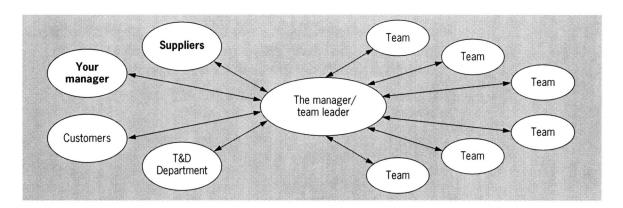

Figure 1.5 *The manager at the hub of a development network*

It is vital that you take advantage of all of the opportunities to engage in a dialogue with these parties to ensure your own and your staff's development needs are aligned with organisational strategy and business plans. This will enable you to determine business, team and individual needs and their priorities. It is especially important that you talk regularly with your suppliers and customers, internal and external (if appropriate), to continue to determine what development is required to meet their needs.

The manager as a developer

So, as a manager or team leader, you have a key role in the development process. You also have a key role in developing your people and facilitating their ability to perform to standard.

The role of developer is highlighted in the following research studies:

> Xerox undertook a major study in the mid 1980s to determine the effectiveness of development and found that 87% of whatever had been learned on training courses was lost within three months of the event.
>
> Bruce Joyce's research in Columbia University suggested that in most training programmes only 13% of learning is transferred to the workplace.
>
> Gers and Seward's longitudinal study found a sustained 92.5% to 97% transfer of learning from courses could be achieved by establishing clear objectives, introducing on-job coaching and by planning how to transfer learning to the workplace.

Source: *Lambert* (1996)

How often do people in your organisation go away on a training course, return enthused, but soon find that it's back to the same job? There is often no effort to bring the learning from training courses back to the workplace. The manager clearly has an important role here. In other words, structured, planned workplace coaching ensures effective development and the manager/team leader is at the heart of this – not the training department.

There are four key ways in which you can play an active role in developing staff:

- by enabling people to attain high performance
- by coaching
- by mentoring
- by delegating tasks and responsibility.

These roles can take place within your role as leader.

Examples of the developer role in action:

- Aligning individuals' development needs with those of the team or unit
- Ensuring that organisational policies towards health and safety, quality, product and service development, introduction of information technology systems, and so on, are incorporated into the development plan of your unit
- Discussing individual development needs
- Coaching and mentoring staff to help them improve their performance
- Supporting and facilitating the application of learning from off-job development activities to the workplace
- Delegating tasks to staff
- Reviewing the outcomes of a task
- Evaluating and measuring performance of staff
- Discussing the performance of the unit with internal and external customers
- Discussing your own development needs with your manager.

The activities that follow help you to examine your reasons for investing in development and a framework for supporting your organisational approach to development.

Activity 2
Why invest in development?

Objectives

Use this activity to:

◆ clarify why your organisation is investing in development

◆ consider whether development is linked to the organisation's needs.

Task

1 List the main reasons why your organisation is investing in people development, for example because of new technology/products, etc.

Organisation's reasons for investing in development:

2 Now consider why you undertake development. List reasons that are personal to you – whether they are concerned with work or other areas of your life.

Own reasons for developing yourself:

Organisations invest in development in order to improve business performance. Changes, like those in technologies, customer requirements and competitor activities, mean that organisations need to develop their people so that they have the knowledge, skills and understanding needed to meet future requirements.

Personal reasons for investing in your own development may include some of the following:

♦ A personal desire to know more about a work-related topic, borne out of a real interest. For example, you may enjoy working on a computer, and might want to know more about how an application works.

♦ Own interest – nothing to do with work – perhaps a hobby or sport.

♦ A wish to become better at what you do, for example to become more useful to your team members.

♦ A desire for greater reward, promotion or other form of advancement in your job.

♦ A desire to keep up to date in your profession.

The more you invest in your own development, the greater the sense of personal satisfaction and the potential for reward. These rewards may come in many different forms.

Activity 3
Development in your organisation

Objective

Use this activity to identify your organisation's approach to development. By this we mean how far development is valued, whether it is seen as an investment or cost, and whether all development is linked to immediate or long-term business needs.

Task

1 Use the questions in the following chart to investigate how development is currently viewed in your organisation. You may need to talk to members of your training and development department, if there is one, or with other managers to find the answers.

Approaches to development	Notes

Who has strategic responsibility for development in your organisation?

How is this responsibility delegated? (You may wish to draw an organisation chart to show this.)

Are there clear indications that development is linked to business needs at all levels of the organisation?

How does the development process for an individual work in practice? (Describe a typical arrangement from an individual's viewpoint.)

Is development competency-linked?

How is the development budget allocated? For example, is there a central budget (all costs held within the HR department budget), or a divisional or departmental budget? Or is there a mixture, with costs for core programmes held centrally, and costs for technical development held by divisions or departments?

What proportion of turnover is spent on development?

Is this investment communicated to managers and staff?

What are the most common (not necessarily popular) forms of development undertaken within your:

◆ *organisation?*

◆ *team?*

What are the most productive forms of development undertaken by your team members?

How is the effectiveness of development evaluated?

2   Your responses to the above questions will give you a clear picture of how your organisation approaches development. What is your assessment of the approach taken? Can you identify where changes or improvements can be made?

Assessment of your organisation's approach to development:

Possible areas for improvement:

Feedback

You may want to discuss your findings with colleagues. You could also discuss key issues with your training and development manager, who should have a strategic overview of development and be able to respond to your findings.

Think about the key areas in which you want to make improvement that will impact on your area. Refer back to the examples of the developer role in action. Could any of these strategies and tactics be used to help develop your staff?

◆ Recap

This themes links the development process to organisational objectives.

Examine the links between employee development and the organisation's goals

◆ Organisations need to recognise the need to create close alignment between the goals that are set at corporate level and those that are set at local level. These local goals should be the focus for effort.

◆ Employee development means investing in the technical/ functional skills, personal/knowledge skills and managerial skills required to meet the organisational objectives.

Identify your role as a manager in developing individuals

◆ The development cycle is a useful framework to identify, plan, implement and evaluate development.

◆ The manager's role is to contribute to the learning and development of the organisation, the team and the individual.

Explore the steps involved in the individual, team and organisational development process

◆ It is vital that the manager takes advantage of all opportunities to engage in a dialogue with organisational stakeholders. This will ensure that individual, team and organisational development is aligned with organisational strategy and needs. Stakeholders include managers, customers, suppliers and other departments.

◆ The key ways you can participate in developing staff are:
  - by enabling people to attain high performance
  - by coaching
  - by mentoring
  - by delegating tasks and responsibilities.

 **More @**

Drucker, P. (1974) *Management: Tasks, Responsibilities, Practices*, Elsevier Butterworth-Heinemann
In this classic text, Peter Drucker studies how modern-day managers, whether in business or public service, can perform effectively. The essence of management is performance. It is the management and managers of our institutions – business and government, educational and multinational – that will determine our future.

Stredwick, J. (2000) *An Introduction to Human Resource Management*, Elsevier Butterworth-Heinemann
A comprehensive and wide-ranging text that examines all the major aspects of human resource management in a down-to-earth and practical way. Chapter 8 focuses on performance management and performance agreements.

Torrington, D. and Hall, L. (1998) 4th edition, *Human Resource Management*, Prentice Hall Europe
The book is written from a practical management perspective. It includes full coverage of operational issues and introduces the major academic debates of relevance to the field.

Tyson, S. and York, A. (2000) 4th edition, *Essentials of HRM*, Elsevier Butterworth-Heinemann

Essentials of HRM combines an overview of organisational behaviour with a detailed explanation of human resources management policies and techniques. It also acts as an introduction to the study of industrial relations. Part 3 examines job analysis, defining effective performance including competencies and Part 4 looks at assessing performance and managing careers.

Full references are provided at the end of the book.

2   Leading and coaching

This theme examines how you can maximise the contribution of your teams and the individuals within them. We focus on:

◆ the role your leadership style can play in encouraging development, and

◆ choosing an appropriate style to develop individuals' skills, confidence and commitment.

One of the tools at your disposal is coaching. We will explore two other tools in the next theme on mentoring and delegating. Coaching is recognised as a powerful tool for learning and development. According to Johnson (2001), more than half of the Fortune 500 corporations offer their managers some form of performance coaching. With clear goals and supportive relationships, coaching can be a very effective technique for developing individuals and improving performance.

In this theme you will:

◆ **Explore the role of leadership in people development**

◆ **Identify the leadership style you tend to use and evaluate the effects of your style on the development of your team members**

◆ **Explore the role of coach and how this can be used when developing people**

◆ **Improve your performance as a coach.**

Leading people for competitive advantage

Influential management writers such as Rosabeth Moss Kanter in *The Change Masters* (1985), and Tom Peters and Robert Waterman in *In Search of Excellence* (1982) have stressed the importance of continuous development and creating empowered workers who can take responsibility for their work. They argue that the quality of staff is a key differentiator for organisations – and development can help to deliver the skills, knowledge and understanding that are essential to building competitive advantage for the organisation. As a manager you are well placed to maximise the contribution of your teams and individual staff members.

This theme focuses on the role your leadership style can play in encouraging development. It helps you to choose an appropriate leadership style to develop your people's skills, confidence and commitment.

How people respond to leaders

People respond to leaders in a number of ways and their responses are often influenced by:

- their feelings about themselves and their situation
- their feelings about the leader
- their relationship with the leader
- the style of leadership that the leader adopts.

Some of the factors above will undoubtedly be affected by the organisational and team cultures within which the individual and the leader operate.

The following short case study highlights different styles of leadership and their effect on an individual:

Julie was really happy in her job – the team had been together for nearly two years and everyone worked well together. One of the main reasons for this was Dennis, the team leader, who was a great guy – friendly, approachable and always around to help with problems. He had time for everyone and on the occasions when quality suffered or targets weren't met, it didn't really matter as Dennis always smoothed things over with his boss. The team and their partners socialised regularly.

Because of a new product development project, Julie was transferred to a new team. She immediately felt uncomfortable with Sanjit, her new team leader. Sanjit was pleasant enough, but he was very tight on quality and gave the team a hard time to make sure that they met all standards and targets. The team members all had different interests and didn't socialise very often. Sanjit also spent a lot of his time with his manager and other managers and less time with his team, saying they were perfectly capable of getting on with their jobs without him being around all of the time. Julie wasn't sure about this, although she liked the additional responsibilities she had been given by Sanjit.

From this short case study it is clear that Julie had mixed feelings about her transfer. She got on better with her previous team leader, but she was enjoying her new responsibilities. Over time, maybe after a chat with Sanjit or at her next appraisal, Julie may begin to recognise that her future career will be enhanced by demonstrating that she can do a good job when given additional responsibilities. She will also settle into the new team's way of working. You may be able to relate Julie's experience to your own experience of joining a new team.

Leadership styles

The leadership style you use influences the manner in which you communicate with the team and the degree of control which you exercise over decision making with the team. Figure 2.1 is one well-known model of leadership and shows the range of leadership styles you can adopt.

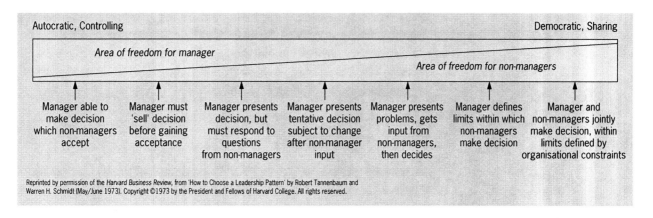

Figure 2.1 *The leadership Continuum*

Source: *Adapted from Tannenbaum and Schmit* (1973)

You can see from Figure 2.1 that if you make full use of your authority and are directive in your approach by making decisions and announcing these to team members, you give them little freedom of action. If you operate at the other end of the continuum, on the other hand, you give your team members a high degree of autonomy and scope to make their own decisions.

Many managers have a preferred style and feel comfortable operating in one part of the continuum, however, in practice most people tend to use different styles, depending on a number of factors.

Tannenbaum and Schmidt (1973) suggest that there are three main forces which affect the types of leadership that are practical at any time:

- forces in the manager, such as personality, background, confidence in staff, feelings of security in a particular situation

- forces in staff members, such as their experience and readiness to take responsibility, interest in and concern with a situation, desire for independence

- forces in the situation, such as the nature of the problem, the urgency attached to it, the consequences of getting it wrong, the predominant culture and management attitudes towards staff in the organisation.

25

It is important to understand that there is no one best way to make decisions within, or on behalf of, a team. A good leader will assess the needs in each situation and, within a relatively short space of time, may operate at opposite ends of the continuum. The leader must also communicate effectively with the team at all times. People should understand a manager's motivations for making decisions if channels of communication remain open and are used appropriately. For example, you may choose to operate at the autocratic/controlling end of the continuum when there are cases of urgency, safety, specialist knowledge, or regulatory or quality standards that cannot be compromised. It is always worth considering the impact of your style on your workload and on the attitudes of individuals and teams.

Who knows best?

How many people report to you? The number of people reporting to a particular manager is called the span of control. In the early 1950s, a leading authority on organisation, Lyndall Urwick (1952), suggested that the span of control should be no more than five or six people.

Technological advances, particularly automation and information technology, coupled with flatter, delayered, organisational structures, has tended to increase managers' span of control. For example, managers at Chrysler in the US at the beginning the 1980s had a span of control of 20, by the 1990s it was 50 and was set to rise again (Crainer, 1998). This increase in span of control means devolved decision making, with workers being encouraged and motivated to take responsibility for the task.

The more people you have reporting to you, the less able you are to retain close control over the work of your subordinates – especially if you want to go home at night. The implication of this is that organisations and managers must devolve decision making, encouraging workers to take responsibility for the quality of their work. They are closest to the job, know it better than you do and are best placed to make decisions about it. Consider the following:

> When doctors listen to nurses, patients recover more quickly; if mining engineers pay more attention to their men than to their machinery, the pits are more efficient. As in athletics and nuclear research, it is neither books nor seminars from which managers learn much, but from here-and-now exchanges about the operational job in hand.

Source: *Revans* (1996)

The idea that employees tend to know their job best has a resonance with employees themselves. They tend to expect and welcome

26

consultation. The post-Second World War baby boomer generation gave way to Generation X (people born between 1965 and 1981) and we now have Generation Y (1978–1994) in the workforce. Writers such as Douglas Coupland (1996), Jay Conger (1998) and more recently Cates and Rahimi (2001) have described the generational differences in workers' expectations. From their research and analysis, it seems clear that workers today tend to be less willing to take straight directions and instructions than their predecessors. They want to know why they have to do something; they want to be consulted.

As a manager, then, you are likely to want to use your leadership style so that people are encouraged to become more self-managing and autonomous in their work and decision making. Your role is to facilitate work – providing support and assistance whenever required.

Using leadership styles to develop staff

Hersey and Blanchard's situational model of leadership style (1993) is concerned with the needs of the tasks and the people who must carry them out. Managers can use the model to diagnose these needs and adapt their style to suit the situation – see Figure 2.2.

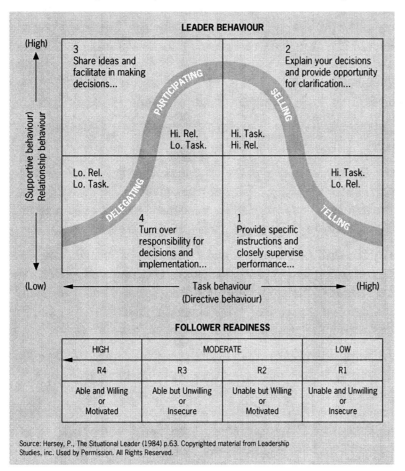

Source: Hersey, P., The Situational Leader (1984) p.63. Copyrighted material from Leadership Studies, inc. Used by Permission. All Rights Reserved.

Figure 2.2 *Situational leadership styles*   Source: *Hersey* (1984)

The model shows that a manager's leadership style for attempting to influence team members is a combination of task behaviour and relationship behaviour:

- Task behaviour is the extent to which the manager needs to focus on the task by providing direction and control over the work. High task behaviour involves a high level of control and direction from the manager.

- Relationship behaviour is the extent to which the manager needs to support, listen, provide encouragement and engage in two-way communication. High relationship behaviour suggests the manager is focusing on people – interpersonal relationships.

The leadership style adopted will depend on the readiness of staff members or groups to carry out a particular task. This readiness is characterised by two factors:

- their competence or level of development
- their motivation and willingness to tackle a particular task.

The motivation and willingness factor may be related to intrinsic aspects of the job – whether it is seen as worthwhile, for instance. However, it is reasonable to assume that if the working environment is not conducive to increasing levels of commitment – for example, if staff perceive there are no rewards for taking on new responsibilities – then motivation and willingness will not increase.

The combination of the two factors suggests four key leadership styles:

Style 1: Directing. Individuals and groups who have a low level of development and low motivation for the task need careful direction, and the manager has a high level of control – for example in setting objectives, planning, monitoring, reviewing and evaluating.

Style 2: Coaching. This style is appropriate for people who are willing to take on a task, but have low to moderate competence. The manager needs to direct and monitor performance, but at the same time to focus on supporting staff – agreeing objectives, discussing and explaining the task and how it can be carried out.

Style 3: Supporting. As people develop, the manager is likely to be able to step back from taking control. Staff may have the competence needed to do the job but as they are taking more responsibility for its completion, are likely to be low in confidence and apprehensive. Here the manager needs to provide a high level of support to encourage and facilitate individuals and teams in making their own decisions.

Style 4: Delegating. As teams and individuals gain experience in taking responsibility and do so successfully, their willingness and motivation increase. Managers can give them responsibility for carrying out the job. They can stand back, but be available to lend general support and specific assistance.

The situational model highlights that to maximise the contribution from individuals and teams, you can modify your leadership style from 1 to 4 to help develop competence and confidence.

Leadership and group decision making

As your teams become more competent and willing, they are likely to become self-managing and able to take decisions as a group. The quality of group decisions may improve as the team becomes aware of the way it makes decisions, and also because of the possibility of the following:

♦ the availability of more information and expertise to inform the decision

♦ fewer errors in using information

♦ the generation of more ideas and alternatives

♦ fewer instances of individual bias

♦ appropriate assessment of risks.

As a manager you will tend to stand back from the group or team and allow it to make its own decisions. However, your role is not wholly hands-off, it may involve offering consultation, facilitation and support. A key part of your role is to help the team enhance its group decision making. Table 2.1 lists common symptoms that inhibit effective group decision making and the preventative measures that you can take.

Symptom of a problem in group decision making	Preventative measures you can take
Illusions of group invulnerability	Encourage open expressions of doubt
Collective rationalism	Accept criticisms of your opinions
Belief in the inherent morality of the group	Encourage high status members of the team to offer opinions last
Stereotypes of other groups	Elicit the opinions of other groups
Direct pressures on dissenters	Periodically divide into sub-groups
Mindguards	Assign a member to be devil's advocate
Self-censorship	Get reactions from outsiders
Illusions of unanimity	Invite outsiders to join discussions periodically

Table 2.1 *Leadership role in enhancing group decision making*

Source: *Jennings and Wattam* (1998)

In the practical activities that follow you will look at your current leadership style and your approach to leadership. You will also be able to carry out a survey of your team's views on development. The final activity provides a development planning approach to use with your team.

Activity 4
Leading people for competitive advantage

Objective

Use this activity to consider your approach to leadership and the styles you currently tend to use.

Task

1 Make copies of Tannenbaum and Schmidt's leadership continuum, which appears in Figure 2.1, for yourself and your team members.

2 Consider your own approach as a team leader and place three crosses (X) on the continuum:

   ◆ Place the left and right X to show the limits within which you believe yourself to be comfortable when dealing with staff situations

   ◆ Place the middle X to show the leadership approach that you believe you adopt in most situations.

3 Give copies of the model to your team members and ask them for their views on your leadership. Ask them to place three crosses as in 2 above. Ask people to undertake this activity individually, without conferring.

4 Evaluate the responses and note differences from your own response. Be open to the responses – remember that other people often see us differently from the way we see ourselves. Give feedback to the team on the consensus in their responses, also noting the extremes of their ranges (if different from the consensus), compared with your own.

   If there are marked differences, seek feedback from the team and ask for examples of behaviours/occurrences which illustrate their views. It is important that the team recognises occasions when you may have to adopt a more autocratic approach.

   It is also important that you are sensitive to the needs of individuals as well as the team. Individuals may have different expectations of you as their leader, and some may be more comfortable with you operating in one mode, rather than another.

5 Think about the effects of your preferred style – bearing in mind the development level of your team and individual team members, and what development is needed. Consider how you might modify your leadership style. You may like to discuss this with trusted colleagues, or seek the guidance of your manager.

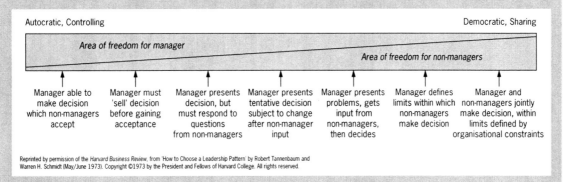

Autocratic, Controlling   Democratic, Sharing

Area of freedom for manager

Area of freedom for non-managers

| Manager able to make decision which non-managers accept | Manager must 'sell' decision before gaining acceptance | Manager presents decision, but must respond to questions from non-managers | Manager presents tentative decision subject to change after non-manager input | Manager presents problems, gets input from non-managers, then decides | Manager defines limits within which non-managers make decision | Manager and non-managers jointly make decision, within limits defined by organisational constraints |

Reprinted by permission of the *Harvard Business Review*, from 'How to Choose a Leadership Pattern' by Robert Tannenbaum and Warren H. Schmidt (May/June 1973). Copyright ©1973 by the President and Fellows of Harvard College. All rights reserved.

Figure 2.1 *The leadership continuum*

Feedback

The diversity of tasks facing today's busy team leaders/managers means that you may have to act autocratically to resolve one situation and be completely democratic in another situation, within the space of a few minutes. However, your overall preferred leadership style will be clearly visible to those people closest to you in the workplace, and their feedback on your style is well worth receiving – even if it doesn't agree with your own perceptions. Consider how far you can maximise the contribution of your team members by modifying your style from controlling to delegating. This may be a key part of your work to develop autonomy in team members and to make your work more manageable.

Activity 5
Team development survey

Objective

Use this activity to:

◆ survey your team members for their views on development

◆ analyse the results of the survey

◆ discuss the results with your staff and your manager.

31

Here you need to understand your team's view about development in your organisation. This will help you to identify the strengths and weaknesses of the current process and identify any action you can take to make team development activities more effective.

Task

1 The questionnaire provided here is for you to give to individual team members for them to complete, without conferring with other team members. You could get a response to these questions in one-to-one discussions, but avoid asking them in a group setting as some team members may feel inhibited. It is important to explain the questionnaire's purpose and how you will use the information you discover.

Make sure that your team members understand that development includes a whole range of on-job and off-job activities and events, not just courses.

Survey of attitudes to development

Please write your comments to each question – use additional paper if needed.

Name:

1 How much company-sponsored development have you undertaken in the past two years? List the events/activities and include all development – not just courses.

2 What self-development opportunities have you taken outside of work in the past two years? For example development connected with a hobby or sport, or personal development.

3 What do you consider to be the most effective development event you have undertaken in the past three years?

Why do you rate it so highly?

Survey of attitudes to development

4   What is the least effective form of development you have undertaken in the past three years?

    Why was this?

5   How much of what you learned in your last two development activities/events do you think you are applying in your work? Give a percentage and an example to support this.

    Event 1

    % applied   Example:

    Event 2

    % applied   Example:

6   Is there a clear link between your development and the team/department's goals? In other words, does the development you have undertaken help you to achieve your goals and those of your team/department?

7   When and in what circumstances do you think you learn best? In other words, what sort of learning works best for you and what sort of support do you think you need to get the most out of any development activity or event?

8   To help you and the team perform more effectively, what do you consider to be the development priorities for:

    ◆ yourself?

    ◆ your team?

    ◆ your manager?

2 Evaluate the responses. Consider what you can learn about individual team members' needs from their responses. Look for trends or patterns in the information you get from the responses as a whole. Summarise your findings:

What development activities/events seem to work well?

Where are there problems?

What support do team members need to make the most of development opportunities?

What do team members think are development priorities?

What action can you take as a result of your findings?

3 Discuss the results of the survey with your manager and your team.

Feedback

Your manager may be able to help you to identify your priorities and any action you can take to improve development in your team. Your team will be especially interested in what you can and will do about areas that they believe need attention. You need to pay careful attention to dealing with their expectations. The golden rule is: **Do not promise anything which you do not have the personal authority to agree or deliver.**

Activity 6
Development planning

Objective

Use this activity to carry out development planning with members of your team.

Your organisation may provide forms and a process for doing this. If so, you should adapt the task in this activity to suit. If not, you can use the self-assessment form and process outlined in the task.

Task

Read through this task first and discuss with your manager how best to complete it, and when you should do it.

To identify the development needs of each member of your team, work through the following steps:

1   Meet with each individual or the team and explain the process – see the Notes for Guidance.

2   Give each individual a copy of the Development Plan form overleaf and ask them to complete the Development Needs sections – agree a date by when they should return the completed form to you.

3   Review the forms and make your own notes regarding their comments and your views. If your views differ, consider how you will address this and discuss each area of difference. You may wish to seek advice from your manager or from the training and development department.

4   Arrange meetings with each member of your team to discuss development needs and priorities. Agree outcomes and complete the form.

5   Consolidate individual development plans into a team plan, and discuss individual and team needs with your manager or the training and development manager, as appropriate. With their agreement, you can proceed to the next stage of the development cycle.

Development Plan

Name: Job Title:

List below areas in which you consider you need to be developed in order to perform more effectively. Then provide possible development solutions:

Development Needs (1)   *Possible Solutions* (2)

1

2

3

4

Development Needs (3)   *Possible Solutions* (2)

1

2

3

4

Development Plan continued

Agreed Priority Development (up to 12 months ahead) [4]   *Completion Date* [5]

1

2

3

4

Agreements (as appropriate) to the above: [6]   *Date Completed*

Individual   1

Manager   2

Senior Manager   3

Other Manager   4

Notes for Guidance

The following numbers relate to the numbers on the Development Plan.

1 This part of the form is your assessment of your development needs, based on your understanding of your current role and/or future role(s).

2 Examples of possible development solutions include the full range of development activities, such as:

- reading books/research
- coaching on the job
- assignments
- project experience
- secondment to another team or department
- job swap
- short courses/programmes
- technical/professional qualification.

3 These are development needs that arise from other sources, for example company-induced development, special projects, change events, to meet company or industry regulatory standards (health and safety, quality, etc.).

If you are aware of these needs write them down, or your manager should confirm them at your development discussion.

4 Agreed development is the outcome of the development discussion between you and your manager. If your views and your manager's views differ, this will be covered in the development discussion.

Your manager will have to take into account budgetary considerations and, if appropriate, plan attendance on courses, absences from work, etc.

5 The completion date may be a fixed requirement, for example to receive training on new technology or processes in conjunction with a change project, or it may be notional.

The important point here is to plan for the development to happen by the completion date.

6 The development plan needs to be agreed by you and your manager. But before development can go ahead, agreement is probably required from other sources, for example senior management or the training and development manager. If there are specific technical needs, a specialist's agreement may be needed.

Feedback

The key to development planning is to allow sufficient time to complete the process, to explain it to individuals, and keep them informed of team and department plans and needs. Bear in mind that it can take time to get development plans agreed, and that they may need to be changed if new priorities for the team emerge.

Remember staff expectations and be prepared to deal with them. It is your responsibility to ensure that the agreed individual and team plans (agreed with your manager and the training department) are translated into actions and you should conduct regular reviews to ensure that development planning leads to appropriate development.

The manager as coach

Coaching is the process by which you help a colleague to explore ways of tackling problems or to change their perspective on work issues, leading to an improvement in their ability to perform. Coaching is not just about helping people to improve practical skills it can be used successfully to develop people and help them become more assertive, communicate more effectively and improve their ability to influence others.

Antonioni (2000) identifies two types of coaching:

The most common is called performance management coaching, and this occurs when there is a gap between an individual's current performance and the way she or he should perform. In these cases, the coach is always the one who initiates the conversation. Performance enhancement coaching, on the other hand, occurs when an individual is meeting performance requirements but wants to perform at a higher skill level or desires coaching to build a new skill. In this case, either the coach or the individual can initiate the coaching process. Unfortunately, most managers spend most of their time doing performance management, leaving little time and attention to help high performers enhance their skills.

Source: *Antonioni* (2000)

How people learn

To understand coaching, it is helpful to recognise the links between coaching and the way people learn.

Much research has been undertaken into how people learn and the early work of Kolb (1985) produced the learning cycle, shown in Figure 2.3. This argues that the process of learning, which is usually passive, should be combined with problem solving, which is defined as active learning.

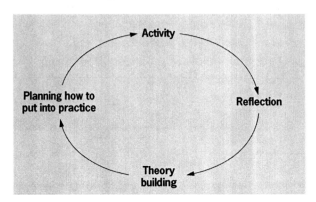

Figure 2.3 *Kolb's learning cycle*   Source: *Adapted from Kolb (1985)*

Each of the four stages of the learning cycle is critical to effective learning. Honey and Mumford (1982) argue that few people are strong in each of the four areas, and that each of us has a preferred learning style:

- **Activists** – learn by doing. These people like to have a go, touch, feel and learn experientially. They may attempt a task with no prior training or knowledge and may be risk takers in the workplace.

- **Reflectors** – prefer to listen and observe. They reflect on and analyse both their own and others' experiences to further their own understanding.

- **Theorists** – build their own understanding through the exploration of theories and concepts. They are also good at integrating different pieces of information to form their own mental models of how things fit together or operate.

- **Pragmatists** – like to use their learning and apply it in a real (work) situation or plan how they can apply it. They often value information in terms of how useful it will be to them in their real world.

It might be construed from Honey and Mumford's descriptions that only one group of people (pragmatists) are naturally predisposed to take their learning and apply it in the workplace. However, the other three groups should also be keen to apply their learning, albeit in different ways.

When you are coaching, it is helpful to be aware of the learning cycle and the preferences for different learning styles people may have. You can build on people's strengths, but you need to ensure that, whatever their preferred learning style, every member of the team converts their learning into practice in the workplace.

The coaching environment

Two key elements within a coaching environment are the learner and the type of workplace in which they work.

The learner

The individual needs to possess a willingness to learn and improve and a willingness to take advantage of the many opportunities that may be available. Above all else, individuals have to take responsibility for their own learning. This means that although the manager and the organisation can provide the environment, support and opportunities, nothing will happen unless individuals have a desire to learn.

Johnson (2001) identifies two groups of people for whom coaching can have positive results:

> First: Strong, talented executive interested in improving her or his decision making, teamwork skills, or other proficiency. Superstars use coaches. Tiger Woods worked intensively with his coach to re-engineer his swing and succeeded spectacularly. Encourage top performers to have a coach.
>
> Second: Someone who is in some kind of trouble at work but wants to salvage the situation and learn what to do. Again, we see great results from this situation. One of the most common is a person who moves from a technical position, such as an engineer, into a supervisory role and doesn't have the people skills to make that work. Classes don't reach the problem like coaching does.

The workplace

A productive workplace is an environment where people are relaxed and feel supported in whatever they do and where mistakes are viewed as an opportunity for learning. This may be seen as a learning environment in which coaching plays an integral part. A learning environment is likely to have the following characteristics:

- People have clear objectives and know how their jobs fit into the bigger picture
- Mistakes are seen as events from which people and the organisation can learn
- Individuals are respected and their inputs to process improvements are encouraged at every level
- Regular feedback is provided, including praise for work well done
- People are encouraged to talk, ask questions and seek clarification
- Collaboration within and across teams is encouraged
- Managers are available to provide advice and assistance when needed.

This case study illustrates coaching in action:

Sally was the new team administrator. It soon became evident that she was uncomfortable with some computer applications, although she had passed tests on them at the recruitment agency. Of particular concern was her apparent unwillingness or inability to file electronic correspondence and find it when asked by her team. In addition, any material initiated by her on behalf of the team often went astray.

Her boss discussed this with her and Sally admitted that although she could type, print correspondence and send e-mails, she had never been trained or learned how to operate an electronic filing system. She was frightened to mention this in case she was sacked in her probationary period. Although her boss was busy, he spent the first 20 minutes every day for one week demonstrating how the applications worked. In the second week, Sally used the system herself but he was on hand to answer queries. One positive aspect of this arrangement was that each morning Sally showed her boss the changes and improvements she had made during the preceding day. At the end of the two-week period, Sally was so confident and competent that she was suggesting improvements to the team's filing system.

The coaching cycle

There are a number of models for coaching but most of them follow the same four basic stages, shown in Figure 2.4.

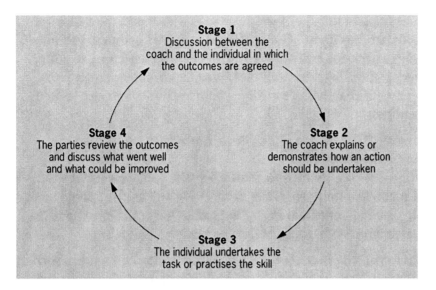

Figure 2.4 *The coaching cycle*

Stage 1: Discussion between the coach and the individual in which the outcomes are agreed

An important element of the coaching process is the development discussion which normally occurs in the first stage of the development cycle. Development discussions should be about determining what development needs have arisen and what may benefit the learner in the future.

These discussions focus on:

◆ gaps in an individual's current competencies that need to be addressed so that they can perform better at work

◆ an individual's career aspirations and options for career development.

Some organisations undertake these discussions as part of the formal appraisal process, combining performance review with development analysis in one interview. Other organisations have separated the two: managers discuss past performance in one interview and future objectives and development needs in a separate interview.

At this stage, make sure that objectives are clearly defined and achievable. Using a simple SMART analysis will help both you and the learner to agree on outcomes.

The SMART acronym is often used to remind us of the recommended features of objectives. You may come across different interpretations of what SMART stands for: Specific or stretching, Measurable, Agreed or achievable, Realistic or results oriented, Time-bound.

Throughout the development discussion process, your role as a coach will be crucial to ensure individuals participate in the next three stages. You may have to explain the rationale for a business need that they do not consider important. Furthermore, you may have to persuade individuals of the benefits of coaching to both them and the organisation; there is little point in arranging development activities for people who are not convinced of their usefulness.

Stage 2: The coach explains or demonstrates how an action should be undertaken

When you coach someone, remember that you are working in a partnership until learners can do the tasks themselves. Avoid being judgemental, impatient or finding fault. One of the most valuable characteristics of a good coach is patience.

Many coaching interventions take place in informal settings such as walking to the car park or over lunch. These informal encounters often amount to no more than a brief chat between individuals, in which one or more of the elements of the cycle are discussed. Antonioni (2000) favours this approach:

> Coaching is a process that works best when it occurs daily; it should not be a formal event that happens only a few times a year. It is not about giving a performance review or an annual appraisal. Most coaching conversations are brief, lasting five to 15 minutes. Brief conversations have more impact, while longer conversations tend to open the door for issue jumping and excessive feedback that can lead to defensive conversations. Short periods of coaching are also more realistic to schedule because they leave time for other high-priority tasks.

Source: *Antonioni* (2000)

Stage 3: The individual undertakes the task or practises the skill

Coaching is not simply a repetitive process. Ideally, the coach starts off in a hands-on role, demonstrating and explaining a task, but eventually assumes a hands-off role. The learner will then assume complete control and feel confident in their command of the task.

Stage 4: The parties review the outcomes and discuss what went well and possible improvements

Giving feedback constructively, so that it does not feel like criticism and thus stimulate a negative reaction, is not easy. It demands a high degree of tact and diplomacy. Holmes (1999) suggests employing the following techniques:

- Discuss specifics and avoid making general statements. Focus on particular areas that went well or need improvement.

- Look for solutions and encourage the learner to develop these for themselves rather than imposing your own ideas.

- Listen more than you talk. Ask the learner to interpret the learning process and share their opinions with you.

- Negotiate new targets that both of you are confident can be achieved within a given period of time.

Above all, you must remain objective and focus on the task or aspect of behaviour that can be improved rather than the characteristics of the person.

Antonioni (2000) believes that coaches benefit from knowing each individual's preference for the sequence of positive and constructive feedback.

An informal survey indicated that at least 80 percent of them want to hear constructive feedback first. This is feedback that is designed to help people improve their performance. Yet we tend to assume that most people want to hear positive feedback first. Since performance management coaching involves giving constructive feedback, some individuals may get defensive because the feedback feels like personal criticism. In some cases, coaches need to develop strategies to help individuals learn how to accept constructive feedback in addition to developing an action plan for improvement.

Source: *Antonioni* (2000)

Characteristics of effective coaches

To be an effective coach demands certain skills and attributes, and effective coaches generally share the following characteristics:

- They are people centred – they demonstrate an interest in people and their development

- They look for potential in people, in their skills, knowledge or attitude

- They set and demand high performance standards and expect people to achieve them

- They delegate responsibility and trust people to perform well

- They allow people space to try out new activities

- They operate in an open, approachable, participative style that encourages people to contribute, express their opinions and share experiences

- They are good communicators, able to put over their points clearly

- They are good listeners.

Factors which hinder effective coaching

There are a number of cultural and behavioural factors that hinder effective coaching:

Cultural

- The organisation does not value coaching and therefore does not support managers in their roles as coaches
- There are no organisational processes or programmes to train coaches
- The organisation espouses coaching, but the reality is that it doesn't happen except through the efforts of committed managers
- The organisation has a formal coaching process and advocates it, but manager workload is so high that coaching happens rarely and often only as a reaction to a problem that has arisen.

Behavioural

- There is a lack of trust and little respect between the manager and the staff member who is being coached
- The manager does not make sufficient time to coach staff properly
- The manager may not have explained the need and context for the coaching
- Staff may not be open to learning new skills or acquiring new knowledge
- Staff may lack confidence in their own ability and may, therefore, revert to old ways of operating rather than embrace the new ways
- Staff may not practise their new skills or apply their new knowledge sufficiently often to show improvement
- Some staff may not want to improve.

Who coaches the coach?

Coaches and managers also need coaching. This may be the responsibility of their own line managers or external coaches may be hired to provide specialist support.

Antonioni (2000) suggests a number of ways in which you can improve and expand your coaching role:

- Get the training you need to develop your coaching skills, particularly in listening, interviewing, giving and receiving feedback, negotiating, managing difficult people, and influencing and training individuals with different learning styles.

- Define your role and responsibilities as a coach; this may improve others' willingness to be coached.

- Determine how and when people would like to receive positive and constructive feedback.

- Get a coach for yourself. This will help you to become familiar with the process, you gain professional development in your own weak areas and you learn by observing your coach in action.

- Practise coaching daily by taking advantage of opportunities that present themselves.

- Reflect on your coaching experiences. Ask yourself: What should I have done more of? What should I do less of? What should I keep doing?

- Ask the people you've coached for feedback.

Finally, Antonioni (2000) suggests that you discuss your goals as coach with your manager during your own performance evaluation:

> Managers who have discussed their coaching with their managers reported that they have increased their managers' awareness of the importance of coaching work and the positive outcomes associated with it. As a result, they received recognition and rewards for coaching. Unfortunately, the management of most organizations say that they want managers to coach, but then they don't back their talk up with recognition or rewards. If this is your situation, then you have an opportunity to demonstrate your leadership on this issue.

Source: *Antonioni* (2000)

The activities that follow examine three key elements of coaching: giving and receiving feedback; The coaching process; planning and holding a coaching session.

Activity 7
Giving and receiving feedback

Objective

This activity asks you to:

◆ assess your current skills in giving and receiving feedback

◆ plan to use guidelines for giving and receiving feedback.

Task

1 Assess your skills for giving feedback against the checklist of good practice in the chart that follows. Read each statement and ask yourself how often you do what is described. Tick the relevant box in the adjacent column.

Giving feedback Good practice checklist	Do you do this?		
	Always	Sometimes	Rarely
1 Offer feedback on observed behaviour, not on perceived attitudes	☐	☐	☐
2 Offer a description of what you saw and how you felt, rather than a judgement	☐	☐	☐
3 Focus on behaviour which can be changed	☐	☐	☐
4 Choose which aspects are most important and limit yourself to those	☐	☐	☐
5 Ask questions, rather than making statements	☐	☐	☐
6 Comment on what the individual did/does well, in addition to areas for improvement	☐	☐	☐
7 Before offering any feedback, consider its value to the recipient	☐	☐	☐
8 Be forward looking – encourage the person receiving the feedback to look at what they can do to improve next time	☐	☐	☐

2 Now review your responses. In which areas can you make improvements? Choose up to four areas for improvement and note what you can do to improve.

Areas for improvement	Plan for action

3 Giving effective feedback is just one half of an effective feedback process. You must also use good practice when receiving feedback. Read the good practice statements in the chart that follows, and tick always, sometimes or rarely for each statement.

You may wish to think about this both from your own viewpoint, for example when receiving feedback from your manager, and from the viewpoint of your staff – how they might respond when receiving feedback from you.

Receiving feedback Good practice checklist	Do you do this? Always	Sometimes	Rarely
1 Listen actively – concentrate on what is being said	☐	☐	☐
2 Clarify – make sure you understand what is being said, ask questions and seek specific examples	☐	☐	☐
3 Accept feedback in the spirit in which it is given – there is no need to justify or defend when the other person gives an honest and constructive account of their experiences of what you did or said, even if you disagree	☐	☐	☐
4 Reflect – think about what has been said. Does it sound familiar or is it new feedback?	☐	☐	☐
5 Say 'thank you'. Many people are uncomfortable about providing direct, honest and open feedback and they should be encouraged to do so	☐	☐	☐
6 Take time for further reflection and to determine your considered (rather than instant) reaction to the feedback	☐	☐	☐
7 Consider options for change. Can you change, should you change, do you want to change, how can you change, etc.?	☐	☐	☐
8 Seek further feedback on any changes/improvements that you have instituted	☐	☐	☐

Feedback is a continuous process – ensure you have a feedback session planned for the future; it may help to motivate you to implement/practise a change.

3 Now review your responses. In which areas can you make improvements? Choose up to four areas for improvement and note what you can do to improve.

Areas for improvement	Plan for action

Feedback

You could take this activity further by giving a copy of these good practice checklists to either a close colleague or your manager and asking them to assess your ability to give and receive feedback. Compare their responses with yours. Who knows, you may have been too hard on yourself, or you may have missed an important aspect of giving or receiving feedback (a blind spot) where another individual's views will provide a different and valuable perspective.

You may also like to think about how your team members receive feedback, and about how to develop good feedback practice within your team.

Activity 8
Coaching works

Objective

Use this activity to:

◆ review common areas (not just work areas) where you know coaching works

◆ link coaching opportunities to both yourself and your staff.

Task

1 You may be more familiar with coaching in areas of your life other than work. List some common areas where you know coaching works.

Coaching – has made a difference to:

2 Now look at coaching from your personal work viewpoint. Using the chart provided, list two or three areas where coaching you have received at work has made a difference, and the results (what it was that you got out of it).

Coaching you have received	Results – what you got out of it

3 For one of the successful instances of coaching that you have highlighted, consider the following questions.

Was it enjoyable?

Were the skills and/or knowledge you developed applied in the workplace?

What were the characteristics of the coach that you found most useful?

Did the coach give you ongoing informal reviews or regular feedback?

Coaching is used in many areas of life. Here are some examples:

◆ Sports: coaches take people with little or no knowledge or capability and help them to perform better at all levels – up to world or Olympic champions. Nobody is born a champion, it is a combination of talent, hard work and good coaching.

◆ Hobbies and interests: many people take up hobbies or interests in which they receive advice and support from people with greater knowledge, from expert practitioners to experienced individuals, for example yoga, pottery, gardening, motorcycle riding, painting, etc.

◆ Bringing up children: parents, teachers, older children, grandparents, etc. may all coach young children to help them acquire a wide range of skills and knowledge.

◆ Rehabilitating people following illnesses or accidents, for example nurses, doctors, physiotherapists, counsellors, osteopaths and therapists.

It is worth reflecting on your experiences of coaching – what went well and what you found to be less successful. These reflections can help you in your work as a coach.

Activity 9

Planning and holding a coaching session

Objective

This activity asks you to plan and carry out a coaching session.

Here we use the four stages of the coaching cycle:

Stage 1: Discussion between the coach and the member of staff, in which you agree the outcomes for the coaching session

Stage 2: The coach explains, or may demonstrate, how an action should be undertaken

Stage 3: The individual undertakes the task or practises the skill

Stage 4: The parties review the outcomes and discuss what went well and what could be improved.

Task

1 Select a member of your team who could benefit from coaching. If coaching is new to this individual, you will need to explain what you are doing and why. Consider what your aims are in coaching, for example, 'to enhance knowledge and use of a software application'.

2 Use the coaching record sheet below to plan, run and review your coaching session or sessions with the individual.

Coaching record sheet

Stage 1 *Discussion and planning*	Main points for discussion: Coaching outcomes to be achieved: What resources, equipment, etc. are needed?
Stage 2 *Explain or demonstrate*	What do you need to explain or demonstrate? You may need to demonstrate the task yourself. Think about the steps involved in doing the task. It can help to break the task down into smaller, manageable steps.
Stage 3 *Practise*	Here the individual undertakes the task, sometimes a step at a time. Here are some guidelines for appropriate coaching at this stage: ◆ Be sensitive to people's feelings. They may be apprehensive, nervous, worried, excited, fearful, overanxious to please or succeed, or feel intimidated by the situation and you. In such circumstances, give them time to adjust to the situation and take it slowly. ◆ Don't worry about mistakes or errors; people learn from them. ◆ Stay positive, calm, supportive and pleasant and allow people time to adjust to the coaching process. ◆ Be prepared to give additional explanation and demonstration. ◆ Allow for slow learners – this doesn't mean they will be slow performers. ◆ Confirm that fast learners have grasped all aspects of the learning and not just a few main points. ◆ Reassure and praise the individuals throughout the session, but do it appropriately. This helps a lot with confidence and motivation.

Stage 4 Review	Revisit the agreed outcomes and discuss performance, again breaking it down into steps. Ask questions like the following:
	'How do you think you did?'
	'Where do you consider you can improve most?'
	'What do you have to do to improve?'
	'What aspect of the task gave you the most problems and why?'
	'What aspect of the task did you enjoy most/least and why?'
	Agree how changes/improvements are to be implemented/practised before the next coaching session:

3 When you have completed one cycle of coaching with a team member, reflect on the success of the exercise by asking yourself the following questions.

How closely did you follow the cycle as outlined in the coaching record sheet? Did you amend it to suit your needs better?

Consider how to improve your coaching the next time:

What will you do the same?

What can you improve?

You can use your amended/improved coaching record sheet for all future coaching sessions. Although we recommend that you retain the essence of the four stages of the coaching cycle, you can amend and improve the record sheet and the way you use it to suit you, your learner and the situation.

◆ Recap

This theme looks at the way leadership styles and coaching can contribute to higher performance in the team.

Explore the role of leadership in people development

◆ The leadership style you use influences the manner in which you communicate with the team and the degree of control you exercise over decision making with the team.

◆ Two models of leadership are illustrated: the leadership continuum and the situational model of leadership. Both include consideration of how you act as a leader in different contexts.

Identify the leadership style you tend to use and evaluate the effects of your style on the development of your team members

◆ Your leadership style will reflect your own preferences, the nature of your team and your organisation, and your current situation.

◆ It is important that you are sensitive to the needs of individuals who have a different expectation of their leader. Some may be more comfortable with you operating in one mode more than in another.

◆ Team and individual development is about consultation, support and planning to meet specific needs. By modifying your situational leadership style from 1 to 4 you will help to maximise the contributions from your teams and develop confidence and competence.

Explore the role of coach and how this can be used when developing people

◆ As a coach you need to be aware of an individual's learning style so that you can build on their strengths and develop new learning skills.

◆ The four stage coaching cycle is a useful framework upon which to base a coaching programme.

◆ Coaches tend to be people centred. They look for potential in people, set and demand high performance, delegate responsibilities well and are open, approachable and good listeners.

Improve your performance as a coach

◆ Giving and receiving feedback are skills that are fundamental to the effectiveness of a coach. These still involve providing and receiving feedback on behaviour exhibited and on areas of performance that really matter.

◆ Use the checklist provided for running a coaching session to jog your memory about what outcomes you need to achieve, how you can achieve them, how the skills can be practised and how the session can be reviewed effectively.

 More @

Dixon, R. (2003) 3rd edition, *The Management Task*, Elsevier Butterworth-Heinemann
This book considers the nature of management and the environment in which management operates. The requirements for effective, successful management techniques are explored, covering leadership in Part 2, Chapter 6. It presents a concise overview of a wide range of leadership models.

Mullins, L. J. (1999) 5th edition, *Management and Organisational Behaviour*, Financial Times Pitman Publishing
Taking a managerial approach and demonstrating the application of behavioural science within the workplace, this text emphasises the role of management as a core integrating activity. This is a long-established text that is accessible in style and clear in presentation, making unfamiliar theory relevant and easily understood and showing how it can logically be applied to the world of work.

Parsloe, E. and Wray, M. (2000) *Coaching, Mentoring: Practical Methods to Improve Learning*, Kogan Page
This text focuses on two key techniques for managers today: coaching and mentoring. In all types of organisation, whether public or private sector, authoritarian styles of management are giving way to the use of managerial techniques that help staff to learn by the use of guidance and example.

Tannenbaum, R. and Schmidt, W. H. (1973) 'How to choose a leadership pattern', *Harvard Business Review*, May/June
This is the original article on leadership styles upon which subsequent research has been based. It outlines the model of leadership based on a continuum from autocratic/controlling to democratic/sharing.

American Society for Training and Development –
www.astd.org/astd
Try searching for coaching and leadership on this website. The site includes articles, discussion boards and surveys on key training and development issues.

Full references are provided at the end of the book.

Mentoring and delegating

The practice of mentoring involves an individual acting as a guide, advisor and counsellor to another. Alongside leadership style, coaching and delegating, it forms one of the key development techniques. This theme looks at the function of mentoring, the benefits and drawbacks, and a mentoring model based on six strategies.

The theme also explores delegation. This is a process where one individual assigns responsibilities to a colleague. It is an approach you can take to develop the skills and confidence of your team members. Here we consider the reasons for delegating and you will examine the scope for delegating with your team.

In this theme you will:

- ◆ **Explore the role of mentoring and how it is linked to staff development and improved performance**
- ◆ **Explore the concept of delegation and the links between delegation and staff development**
- ◆ **Identify areas where your effectiveness as a delegator can be improved.**

Mentoring

What is mentoring? There are a number of definitions and here are just a few of them.

Parsloe (1992) suggests that mentoring is:

> ...concerned with the longer-term acquisition and application of skills in a developing career by a form of advising and counselling.

Source: *Parsloe* (1992)

Caldwell and Carter (1993) state:

> Most mentoring partnerships fall into one of two categories: those which emphasise professional development only, and those which include both personal and professional development.

Source: *Caldwell and Carter* (1993)

Mentoring differs from coaching and the two roles should not be confused.

Johnson (2001) states:

> A coach provides specific suggestions about improving your performance; he or she is usually outside the team proper. The coach helps you play the game but is not in the game. A mentor is someone in the game who helps you develop your career. A mentor may have power in the system and can sponsor the protégé into opportunities.

Source: Johnson (2001)

Mentoring can vary according to the context and the purpose for which it is being used, but it has two unique characteristics:

- It is a relationship built on mutual trust, respect and confidentiality
- It facilitates a process of learning, development and experimentation.

Mentoring and its uses

Mentoring has been described as a form of professional intimacy in which the mentor and the protégé form a relationship that lies somewhere in the middle of the colleague-friend continuum. Mentoring can be used in a number of ways, for example:

- in the induction of new staff
- to offer support with educational programmes
- to develop staff who have been identified as having high potential
- to support staff involved in a career change or a significant change in their responsibilities.

There are two forms of mentoring:

- in-line, where the mentor is in the protégé's direct reporting line – the mentor is usually the protégé's manager, but may also be a senior manager
- off-line, where the mentor and the protégé do not have a formal reporting line to each other.

There are benefits and drawbacks for the protégé in both forms of mentoring, as illustrated in Table 3.1.

In-line mentoring	
Benefits	The protégé is usually well known to the mentor
	Easy access to mentor
	Mentoring is regarded as ongoing and is often informal
Drawbacks	The mentor may not be impartial
	There could be accusations of favouritism from other team members who are not being mentored
	Other discussions may be construed as mentoring and there will be insufficient time to discuss wider issues
	Mentor may develop the protégé to perform better in their role rather than for wider/higher positions
	Guarded disclosures – have to think about relationships/appraisals

Off-line mentoring	
Benefits	Encourages networking
	Gives a broader view of senior management, perhaps from other areas of the organisation
	Can speak frankly, openly
	Mentor is impartial and not involved with in-line issues
Drawbacks	Formal time is usually set aside for mentoring
	Limited opportunities to meet
	Mentor may have no understanding of job-related issues
	Mentor may have little or no previous knowledge about the protégé

Table 3.1 *Benefits and drawbacks of mentoring*

Johnson (2001) suggests that if a mentor is only one level above the protégé, this can lead to a conflict of interest.

> The protégé is a potential competitor for the immediate supervisor's position. It is in the selfish interests of the supervisor to keep subordinates from achieving too well, lest the supervisor be replaced ... An effective mentor is at least two levels removed from the protégé. The greater the separation, the greater the potential to the protégé. An effective mentor-protégé relationship has enough separation that the mentor will never feel threatened by strong progress by the protégé.

Source: *Johnson* (2001)

One of the particular attributes of off-line mentors is that they may look out for opportunities for their protégés beyond the confines of their current role. The mentor will balance the needs of the protégé's current department against the broader needs of the organisation as a whole.

What function does mentoring perform?

For the protégé, mentoring can facilitate:

◆ career development through exposure to, and sponsorship by, senior management

◆ personal development by providing a developed sense of competence, effectiveness and identity within the organisation, and through support in learning activities.

The benefits of mentoring

Mentoring benefits the mentor, the protégé and the organisation.

For the mentor

Being asked to act as a mentor is recognition of your leadership skills. If you are acting as an off-line mentor, the gains are particularly great since it will give you the chance to:

◆ promote the organisation's vision, values and strategies and the wider environment within which the organisation operates

◆ gain personal satisfaction through development of people who are outside your own immediate area of responsibility

◆ interact with junior staff from other areas of the organisation.

Protégés can also be a useful source of new ideas and provide assistance on projects.

For the protégé

The benefits of the mentoring relationship include:

◆ enhanced knowledge and understanding of the wider issues affecting the organisation and the impact they have on policies and processes

◆ greater awareness of organisational culture and politics

◆ improved confidence and sense of worth

◆ the provision of a safe learning environment through observation and advice rather than trial and error

- a source of help, support and objective feedback and a sounding board for ideas

- access and visibility to senior management, which offers a source of career and networking opportunities.

For the organisation

Successful mentoring arrangements within an organisation can:

- speed up the induction process for new employees
- develop a culture of co-operation
- improve staff retention rates
- facilitate internal communications
- encourage the development of a learning organisation
- bridge the gap between development and training theory and practice in the workplace
- create a more profound understanding of the organisation's aims, objectives, culture and systems.

Identifying protégés

Someone who will benefit from their role as a protégé will demonstrate the following characteristics:

- a commitment to their own development
- flexibility in their approach to change and the role that they may play within a change situation
- a willingness to be open about their feelings, motivations and ambitions
- receptiveness to new ideas, including alternative career options
- enthusiasm to understand better the broader environment in which they operate
- a willingness to undertake extra study and effort to achieve their goals.

Minter and Thomas (2000) suggest a range of behaviours that potential protégés should display. Mentoring strategies should be initiated if the manager perceives that an employee is meeting approximately 70 per cent of the average performer assumptions that follow:

- Exhibits standard or average performance behaviour on a continuous basis
- Has the capacity and potential to improve the quality/quantity of performance beyond the standard, but needs additional training and experience
- Has the potential to become a strong team player
- Is not yet meeting performance expectations because they are new to the job or organisation
- Requires specific instruction in skill/knowledge areas to develop the necessary abilities and willingness to meet performance expectations
- Requires moderate to close supervision
- Has difficulty assuming higher levels of accountability at this time due to their current state of knowledge or skill/ability levels
- Is not effective at this point in time in managing key responsibilities
- Has potential to be a high performance employee (HPE) in the department/organisation
- Has potential to achieve expected competency levels
- Is unable to bring about improvement on their own initiative
- Requires a manager or designated individual to work side by side with them on selected critical tasks, in order to bring about significant performance improvement
- Needs to demonstrate improvement in selected area to be retained in the current job
- Demonstrates performance concerns that relate more to their knowledge, skill or ability levels than to attitudinal or behavioural problems.

Source: *Adapted from Minter and Thomas* (2000)

Identifying mentors

A good mentor is someone who:

- is recognised as a good leader and team player
- has professional and personal respect from senior management and their peer group
- is familiar with the organisation and its external environments, including network contacts
- is committed to the development of people
- helps the individual to explore possibilities and to develop their confidence.

A mentoring model

Mentoring can take place through an informal arrangement between two members of staff or through a more formal mentoring programme which has been set up to promote learning or support a development initiative. In the latter case, the success of the mentoring depends on support from the organisation.

Minter and Thomas (2000) suggest a mentoring model that can be used in both formal and informal mentoring, based on six strategies:

- identifying critical ability, skill and knowledge deficiencies that require further development
- determining whether the performance deficiencies can be addressed by providing training or non-training solutions
- obtaining understanding and agreement from the employee to correct identified deficiencies
- developing and implementing an action plan to correct specific performance deviations
- measuring performance improvement outcomes on a short and long-term basis
- providing continual feedback to the employee on their progress.

They champion the use of hands-on instruction as an effective teaming approach to facilitate improvement:

Research on employee retention during training reveals that, if a manager tells an employee what to do, he or she will remember approximately 10 per cent of the job instructions. When the manager tells and shows the employee what to do, the employee will remember approximately 60 per cent of the information. When the manager combines tell and show with the employee demonstrating what was observed, the employee will retain approximately 90 per cent of the instructional effort.

Source: *Minter and Thomas* (2000)

This principle can be used in developing a wide range of both hard and soft skills. For example, if a protégé observes you regularly practising time management skills, and you periodically provide feedback about time management practice and its benefits, the principles will be reinforced and your protégé will be encouraged to practise these skills for themselves.

The mentoring life cycle

A mentoring relationship will follow a cycle of birth, growth, maturity and conclusion. The key elements of these phases are shown in Table 3.2.

Birth	Mutual identification of mentor/protégé
	Gaining commitment to the process
	Establishment of objectives, processes and ground rules
Growth	Getting to know each other better
	Focusing on strategies and tactics to achieve objectives
	Working together
	Building/achieving trust
Maturity	Learning together
	Reviewing progress
	Re-evaluating objectives
	Redefining processes and fine tuning roles
Conclusion	Final review of achievements against objectives
	Summary of learning gained
	Ending of the relationship on a positive note
	Development of protégé independence

Table 3.2 *Key elements of the mentoring life cycle*

Delegating

Delegation involves:

- giving responsibility to another person for the completion of a task for which you are accountable
- giving that person the authority and resources to carry out the task without constantly referring back to you for approval or clearance.

It is important to distinguish between delegation and abdication of responsibility. We can delegate authority to others to act on our behalf, for example by signing orders and invoices, but ultimately we can't delegate responsibility or accountability for tasks that are within our remit.

Rosabeth Moss Kanter (1988) highlights this difference:

> Delegating responsibility to other people does not mean abdicating managerial responsibilities for monitoring and supporting the process. Some managers assume an either/or world where either they are in complete control or they have given up all control. But delegation – whether by a management team to a set of employee teams or by a single manager to his or her subordinates – means that the manager not only sets the basic conditions but also stays involved, available, to support employees, reviewing results, redirecting or reorienting the team as necessary.

Source: *Kanter* (1988)

An example of poor delegation was the 'burying bad news' incident in the UK in September 2001. Transport Secretary Stephen Byers delegated authority to brief the press to his special adviser, Jo Moore, but when she made an error of judgement he found that he was accountable for what she did – and his job was under threat. Ultimately managers are always responsible for the actions of their staff, even though they give staff the authority to take action.

Thomson (1998) cites a number of factors that affect how much authority you, as a manager, should delegate:

- The size of the organisation – the larger the organisation, the more decisions have to be made and the more tasks undertaken; managers in large organisations have to delegate to get things done

- The importance of the decision – the more important the decision, the less likely it is to be delegated

- Task complexity – complex tasks which require expert or technical knowledge need to be delegated to those who can best perform them

- Organisational culture – there needs to be a culture of mutual trust between managers and subordinates to support effective delegation

- Quality of subordinates – delegation requires subordinates with the skills and ability to accept delegation.

The emerging trend in delegation

In recent years, the delayering of organisations into flatter structures with fewer layers of management has increased the need for effective delegation. Delayering has hit the ranks of middle managers hardest and, in an effort to protect themselves, the survivors may feel they need to hold on to their responsibilities and authority rather than delegate. Taking this approach has two main drawbacks:

- Managers quickly become swamped by their responsibilities and do not work effectively
- Valuable development opportunities are lost as junior staff have fewer chances to take responsibility.

The components of effective delegation

There are three strands to effective delegation.

1 Knowing what to delegate

Some managers may delegate simple, routine tasks and then closely supervise the people undertaking them. At the other end of the continuum, managers may delegate tasks and responsibility to staff and pay very little attention to how the tasks might be achieved.

There are some areas where a manager has to retain authority in order to comply with policies and with regulatory and legal requirements. If you are unsure about how much authority you should delegate, the best approach is to delegate in stages. Provided staff meet all objectives for previously delegated tasks, then their levels of responsibility and authority can be increased. Giving people more responsibility and authority than they are comfortable with can be counterproductive since too much of your time will be spent in coaching, reassuring or checking them.

2 Trusting your staff and being willing to show this trust

As the responsible manager, you ultimately 'carry the can' for anything that occurs or does not occur within your area of responsibility. Therefore, although you may delegate the task, you retain overall responsibility for its completion. Managers therefore tend to delegate to people whom they trust, and the degree of control they exercise is directly related to the level of trust they have in the individual or team to perform the task effectively.

Delegation is about relinquishing control and showing trust in others. Managers often ask others to do a task but retain authority for it, suggesting that they lack confidence or trust in their subordinates. This approach is taken so that staff understand that the power still lies with the manager – this is not true delegation.

3 Timing

Staff do not all operate at the same level and will be at different stages of personal and professional development. Consequently, the timing of delegation is important. Managers must gauge each individual's capacity to receive additional responsibilities and the manner in which these responsibilities can be handed over. Experienced members of staff may need no more than an informal chat and agreement on what is expected, whereas other members of staff may need detailed written instructions and coaching before they can accept new responsibilities.

The benefits of effective delegation

Effective delegation can benefit you, your staff and the organisation as a whole:

- You gain more time to complete tasks that you cannot delegate
- You can reduce your workload and stress levels
- You can take a broader view of the work of your department and the ways in which your staff interact
- Your staff develop their own skills, judgements and sense of responsibility
- Your staff become more involved in their work and thus better motivated
- Increased motivation can lead to a reduction in staff turnover and costs related to recruitment and induction
- The organisation can identify potential managers and high-flyers.

Barriers to effective delegation

Delegation involves risk. If you delegate a task and the person who takes it on does not complete it adequately, then you will carry the responsibility for its failure.

The amount you delegate reflects your management style. Some people will feel more comfortable with little delegation, perhaps because they don't trust people or they have a high need for power, whereas others will be only too happy to delegate a large slice of their responsibilities across their team.

This list suggests some common barriers to effective delegation. You could use it as a checklist to identify your own willingness (or reluctance) to delegate.

- You lack confidence in your staff and feel that there is no one to whom you can delegate
- It's quicker to do the job yourself than to train or monitor others
- You fear that your staff are too inexperienced and will not cope with the responsibility of delegated tasks

- You are afraid of losing control and being declared superfluous
- You work in a hierarchical culture where delegation is not encouraged or where managers are seen as controllers
- You want to delegate, but your staff need training which isn't readily available.

If you recognise any of these barriers to delegation in your own performance, think about how you can overcome them. You may need to address training needs in your department; you may also have to address your own beliefs about yourself and your colleagues. Talk to your own managers about ways in which levels of delegation can be improved.

The delegation process

To delegate effectively, you need to follow a structured approach. This is not something that can be done on the spur of the moment. If staff to whom you delegate are inadequately prepared or unclear about what their new role involves, they will not perform satisfactorily.

In setting up a system for successful delegation, Mullins (1999) suggests that managers should consider these questions:

- What tasks could be performed better by subordinates?
- What opportunities are there for subordinates to learn and develop by undertaking delegated tasks and responsibilities?
- How should the increased responsibilities be implemented and to whom should they be given?
- What forms of monitoring control system would be most appropriate?

Mullins also states:

In order for a delegation system to work effectively, staff should know exactly what is expected of them, what has to be achieved, the boundaries within which they have freedom of action and how far they can exercise independent decision-making.

Source: *Mullins* (1999)

The following steps form the basis of an effective delegation process.

1 Identify the tasks that can be delegated

Start by considering **what** you can delegate. Factors to consider include the following:

- Avoid delegating tasks that are urgent or have to be completed in a hurry since you will not have time to work through the delegation process
- The task should be worth doing, so that the person you ask to complete it develops a sense of ownership and pride in carrying out the work
- You should not delegate any task that carries statutory or legal implications, or which your superiors expect you to do yourself
- Do not delegate tasks that could create dissent within your department, for example it would be inappropriate to ask one team member to take on a job that involves dealing with the confidential files of other team members.

2 Allocate the tasks to the right people

The next step is to identify **to whom** you can delegate a task. A large part of successful delegation rests on matching the right person to the right task. Consider whether the person you want to take on the job:

- has a workload that allows them to carry out extra work
- has indicated that they want more responsibility
- has some background experience that is appropriate to the task
- is willing to undertake training if necessary to complete the task.

3 Brief the person or people involved

When you have selected the task and the person to whom you want to delegate it, you need to prepare a brief that states clearly what should be achieved. The length and comprehensiveness of the brief will depend on the confidence and experience of the person who is taking on the task.

When you explain the task, make it clear:

- why the task is necessary
- what should be achieved
- what the person you have approached will gain from it in terms of experience and satisfaction

♦ what authority and resources are being delegated

♦ where they can get help if they need it.

Although the brief should be clear, you do not need to spell out how the job should be done. Delegation involves letting people take ownership of a task and therefore finding their own ways in which to complete it. You should, however, be willing to offer suggestions if they are asked for, discuss ideas and provide feedback.

4   Support and monitor performance

During the period when the task is carried out, you should offer support, if it is needed, and monitor the task or project to make sure it stays on track. The extent to which you get directly involved will depend on how much you trust your staff, how well they are responding to the challenge and how much you can bear to stand back. Ideally, you will keep your distance and only get involved if you are asked to. Constant interference negates the whole delegation process.

5   Give feedback

Once the task is completed, review it with the person to whom it was delegated. In this way you 'close the loop' by using the experience as a learning exercise. In particular, consider:

♦ what went smoothly

♦ any problems that arose

♦ how the person you delegated to responded to the challenge

♦ further opportunities for delegation that could arise in the near future.

Activity 10

Delegation and decision making

Objective

Use the case study in this activity to identify opportunities for delegating.

Task

1   Read the following case study.

Sarah had recently been promoted to the operations manager of a very busy call centre, providing 24/365 (24 hours per day, every day of the year) cover to bank customers. The centre employed 650 call operators on shifts. Her previous job was administration manager. The call centre dealt with a wide range of routine enquiries, mainly relating to customers' accounts and also dealing with potential customer enquiries from people responding to advertising campaigns. New customers were especially valuable, as the company knew it could eventually sell them at least three other products, in addition to the product which had caused them to phone in, thereby exponentially increasing income over the customer life cycle. Although no outgoing canvassing calls were made to customers, every incoming call was also treated as an opportunity to sell more products and services. Every call operator and supervisor had challenging weekly targets which they had to achieve, including passing on callers to sales staff.

The role of the operations manager was to ensure that all support functions ran smoothly, and also to provide constant cover to the call centre operators. The prime responsibilities were for the computer and telephone systems. Sarah was responsible for two managers and eight supervisors, who ran the telephone and computer maintenance teams, as well as a premises manager, an administration support manager and three supervisors for the administration team. Her key customer is the call centre manager, who is her peer and they both report to the national calls division director, who is located in the same building. The call centre manager is responsible for product and service delivery, including customer services, and the profitability of the call centre. Both managers have quality and service delivery standards which they must meet.

The job was hectic and, although Sarah normally worked days, she was often in early and still at her desk late in the evenings; the long hours were taking their toll on her and she was beginning to feel tired all of the time. She kept telling herself that once she got the hang of it, she would cut down on her hours and phone her friends whom she had 'put on hold'.

Because of the state-of-the-art telephone and computer systems, very little planned maintenance was undertaken, but the wear and tear on the building from the 24-hour staff coverage meant there was always a part of the building or phone and computer equipment under repair or refurbishment. Where possible, much of this work took place between 10.00pm and 6.00am when the call load was lighter and fewer staff were on the night shift.

Tuesday began as a normally busy day, with a team briefing with all of her managers. Sarah knew she still had a lot to learn about running team briefings. Hers had always been a bit haphazard and she knew she talked too much, the result being that she didn't receive as much information as she should about what was happening around the department. No special incidents had been reported by her managers, other than the computer manager reporting that the three-second access time to retrieve a customer record after asking for their postal code was not being achieved and the incidence of longer time taken was increasing. Furthermore, both his and the product supplier's software engineers didn't understand why this was happening. This really worried Sarah as the company made great play about this response time in its marketing campaigns. The meeting was then interrupted by a telephone systems supervisor to say that the system had gone down and no incoming calls were being received. Although he wasn't certain, it appeared the fault was in the call queuing system which was rejecting rather than stacking calls. This was a serious situation, especially with potential new customers – people would be likely to take their business elsewhere if they couldn't get through to the company. Sarah abandoned the meeting and went with the telephone manager and the supervisor to find out more about the problem. At the same time, her PA was trying to get hold of her because her boss needed to talk with her urgently – maybe someone had already told him about the problems with the phone system.

On her way to the telephone systems computer, Sarah was asked by the administration manager, who was walking along with her, about the supervisor interviews which she and Sarah were due to conduct later in the morning. Sarah said that she would be available. While in the telephone systems office, Sarah received a call from her PA asking her to ring her boss and also asking her to speak urgently with the premises manager. The PA was frustrated because Sarah wasn't using her properly and she often didn't know where Sarah was in the building. It seemed that the premises manager needed an urgent response to a query which he had been going to raise at the abandoned meeting – he needed to shut off mains power for five minutes and this would mean cutting in the emergency power system. Although the company had a special system in place to smooth out power fluctuations on changeovers from mains to emergency power, the last two times this had operated, severe computer problems had arisen and it had taken two days of hard work to recover the situation.

It never rains, but it pours. On her way back from the telephone systems department, still with no solution in place, Sarah bumped into her boss who said he needed to speak with her regarding her draft budget submission which was overdue, and which he needed to fit into his divisional budget. He also asked Sarah if she was OK as she looked tired and worried. Just then, the call centre manager appeared and asked, 'What's happening?' which really meant, 'Nothing is happening and what are you doing about it?'

Sarah explained her current problems to her boss and said that she would get the budget to him soon, but overriding operational issues were taking her time at the moment. Much of the budget work had been undertaken by Sarah in her previous role of administration manager and she had taken this task with her on the basis that she knew more about the budgeting process than her successor. The boss's response was to tell Sarah that, having promoted her into the position, he expected her to deliver results and manage her problems. Having said that, he calmed down and suggested he and Sarah take time out to review the current situation and her workload to see what she could and should do.

2   What do you consider Sarah's manager may suggest? Write your suggestions below. Put yourself in Sarah's position, think about the issues she is facing and provide sound, common-sense suggestions relevant to her situation and work environment.

What Sarah could and should do:

Feedback

This case study is about delegation and decision making. Sarah is working long hours because she feels she needs to get to grips with the broad scope of her job, or perhaps because she is not getting to grips with her new job! However, you may agree that being tired at work and dropping friends because of work are not the answers. Sarah seems to be keen to take control, but can't do it all. She should delegate most operational issues to her managers and their teams; from what we know, they all appear to be competent individuals.

The job of Sarah's managers is to run their areas of responsibility, keep Sarah informed and, on important issues, present her with options and recommendations. Sarah can then make a decision or, if necessary, discuss the issue further with the manager and team involved, and possibly with her manager or the call centre manager.

Here are some specific suggestions.

Sarah could:

- Ask the telephone systems manager to provide her with a current update and present her with a worst-case scenario which she would need to take to her manager. The company should have a contingency plan for such occurrences, including re-routing calls to other centres. Her manager will probably need to be kept fully informed of developments because of the implications of workloads on other centres and absence of work for local staff. She should also discuss the situation immediately with the call centre manager.

- Ask the computer systems manager to continue to liaise with the product engineers to find and rectify the fault in accessing customer files. The computer systems managers should also ascertain whether this was a local, one-off fault or whether it had occurred elsewhere, maybe within another company using the same software.

- Keep the call centre manager informed of developments and determine how the call operators are dealing with disgruntled callers who mention the delays.

- Brief the new administration manager and let her complete the budget, otherwise she will not be well placed to complete next year's budget. Sarah should be available to offer advice and support if needed. She should then scrutinise and approve the budget submission before passing it to her manager.

- Speak with the premises manager to find out why he needs to shut down mains power. Unless this is a critical issue, it should be deferred until other problems have been rectified.

Furthermore, she should determine what had occurred to rectify the previous power fluctuations when transferring to standby power. Was this likely to reoccur and would the implications be the same as before? Until she knows the answers to these questions, the power must stay on.

♦ Plan to get some support in developing her team-briefing skills.

Activity 11
Delegation in your workplace

Objective

Use this activity to:

♦ consider the reasons for delegating and for accepting delegated tasks

♦ explore the scope for delegation in your team or department.

Task

1 Give three reasons why you should accept delegated tasks from your manager.

1

2

3

2 Now consider which tasks your manager currently delegates to you and whether there is scope for more delegation to you.

Manager delegation

Tasks currently delegated

How much responsibility/authority is assigned to you for this task?

Tasks that could be delegated

How much responsibility/authority could be assigned to you for this task?

3 Finally, consider the tasks you delegate to team members and whether there is scope for further delegation.

Delegated tasks

Tasks currently delegated to team members	*Name of team member*	*How much responsibility/authority is assigned to the team member for this task?*
Tasks that could be delegated	*Name of team member*	*How much responsibility/authority could be assigned to the team member for this task?*

Discuss the above issues with the team members involved, and also with other team members who do not currently have delegated tasks to determine their willingness to accept them. They may also have some insights as to which tasks they would willingly accept – or not!

Feedback

There are a number of good reasons why you should accept delegated tasks, including:

♦ The task may be unusual or different. It may broaden your understanding and capability in another area (i.e. it is developmental).

♦ The manager may want to see how you respond to the task – both your demeanour and how well you perform it. (They may be checking you out for other possibilities.)

♦ Your manager may have a heavy schedule and the only way he or she can achieve multiple tasking is to delegate. Provided you achieve a positive outcome, your willingness to help out will be well regarded.

♦ Your manager may have decided to concentrate on other tasks and believe that this particular task is within your capability.

♦ You may possess special skills or knowledge (perhaps not shared by your manager) which makes you the obvious choice for a particular task.

♦ Finally, your willingness to accept delegated tasks will indicate that you are a good team player, able to cope with additional, sometimes ad hoc, work and are able to work beyond your normal job – all good indicators of potential.

If you have completed this activity conscientiously, you should have clarified a few issues and perhaps made life easier for yourself and others. Remember that in delegating new tasks, you should take the time to explain clearly what the task is and why you are delegating it, together with the outcomes you wish to achieve. Most people react well to effective delegation – give them the opportunity to show you what they can do.

◆ Recap

This theme examines the key processes surrounding mentoring and delegating.

Explore the role of mentoring and how it is linked to staff development and improved performance

◆ Mentoring is the longer-term acquisition and application of skills in a developing career by a form of advising and counselling.

◆ Mentoring is used to develop the careers of individuals by increasing their competence, effectiveness and identity within the organisation through learning activities and support. The mentor, the protégé and the organisation are all likely to benefit from the experience.

Explore the concept of delegation and the links between delegation and staff development

◆ Delegation involves giving responsibility to another person for the completion of a task for which you are responsible, whilst providing them with the authority and resources to carry it out.

◆ In order to delegate you need to know what to delegate, be able to show that you trust the person you delegate to and be sure the person you delegate to has the capacity to receive additional responsibilities.

◆ Delegation means briefing the people involved, supporting and monitoring performance and giving feedback to ensure that any learning points are captured and worked on.

Identify areas where your effectiveness as a delegator can be improved

Barriers to effective delegation include:

◆ lack of confidence in staff

◆ the feeling that it's quicker to do the job yourself

◆ fearing that staff are too inexperienced and not recognising the potential for development in team members

◆ fearing that you might lose control

◆ organisational culture.

 **More @**

Parsloe, E. and Wray, M. (2000) *Coaching, Mentoring: Practical Methods to Improve Learning*, **Kogan Page**
This text focuses on two key techniques for managers today: coaching and mentoring. In all types of organisation, whether public or private sector, authoritarian styles of management are giving way to the use of managerial techniques that help staff to learn by the use of guidance and example.

American Society for Training and Development –
www.astd.org/astd
Try searching for mentoring and delegating on this website. The site includes articles, discussion boards and surveys on key training and development issues.

Bized – www.bized.ac.uk/homeinfo/sitemap.htm
Try searching for articles and learning resources on this business education website.

Full references are provided at the end of the book.

4   Change and performance

Change and learning are inextricably linked. Learning brings about change in people and organisations. Organisations seek to learn – to become learning organisations – so they can both foresee the need for new products and new operations and be flexible and change-ready when change is required. This theme looks at the links between change and development.

Managers have a key role in facilitating learning and development in their teams. Here we look at competencies and why they are important. Competencies focus on the performance required – what people need to be able to do. You will be able to review how organisations can use defined competencies to develop the skills of the workforce for the future and to keep pace with change.

In this theme you will:

◆ **Explore ways of finding development opportunities when tackling change**

◆ **Identify how employee competencies can be linked to high performance.**

The challenge of change

We know that people learn from daily activity, from reflecting on their experiences, and from developing an understanding of the way things work. Kolb's learning cycle demonstrates this process – see Figure 4.1.

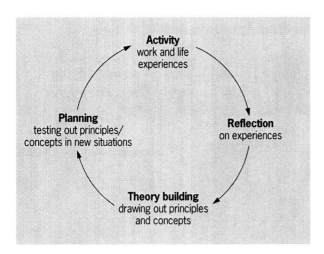

Figure 4.1 *Kolb's learning cycle*   Source: *Kolb* (1985)

The cycle shows that learning is about gaining experience, which over time gives us the mental models that we then use when tackling new problems. We take positive steps to check out these mental models, then take action using these models. The Kolb cycle contains two important messages when we are looking for development opportunities in a situation of change:

- People prefer to focus their learning, and hence development, at different stages in the cycle. The focus for many people is around action taking and they then spend very little time on the other stages.
- The value that is attributed to learning from the various stages of the cycle will depend on the work context and the experience of the individual in that job.

Opportunities for development occur whenever the team faces change, be it incremental or radical. As a manager, you can encourage staff to use the learning cycle by using the stages when leading the team in problem-solving, task-setting and review situations.

Reg Revans (1982), another well-known writer on change and learning, makes the following important points about learning and change:

- When individuals are learning faster than the changes are occurring, then they stay ahead of the game
- When events change faster than individuals can learn, they will eventually be unable to respond.

In the latter case, where change is greater than learning, individuals will tend to avoid opportunities to learn and their development and performance will be damaged as a result.

As a manager, your job is to help your staff use change as an opportunity to learn and develop, and to prevent them from becoming submerged by the learning that is required. Sir John Harvey-Jones, former Chief Executive of ICI, states:

Management is not about preserving the status quo, it is about maintaining the highest rate of change that the organisation and people within it can stand.

Source: *Harvey-Jones* (1990)

Linking development and change

Here is an example of how change and development were linked in one organisation.

A large engineering company had an old mainframe computer with terminals in every office. The mainframe had many limitations and, as the costs of upgrading it outweighed the benefits, the company decided to invest in PC technology with servers/desktop terminals. This meant that every design engineer (some three hundred staff) would have their own PC on their desks rather than one mainframe terminal per workstation of four to six people. Top end computer-aided-design (CAD) PCs were also purchased and placed on each group of workstations so the engineers could make use of them when needed. The company fully understood that the design engineers would need to learn how to operate the CAD system, and a training programme was planned and implemented. However, what it had not fully understood was the flexibility and potential afforded to the engineers by the Microsoft® Windows and Office software applications on the PCs.

Individuals began to write their own letters, compile their own spreadsheets and plan their own presentations. This meant secretaries, desk-top publishing (DTP) support staff and design assistants were not doing as much work as previously because the engineers found it quicker and simpler to do it themselves.

To maximise this opportunity, the company implemented a wide-ranging series of self-learning packages on the applications in which the engineers learned at their own pace. Secretaries were re-skilled as team administrators, and design assistants absorbed other design functions. The company also conducted a cost–benefit analysis, to ensure that design engineers were not being distracted from their primary function, and found that overall productivity had improved.

Change – an opportunity

When an individual moves to a new or different situation, there is an opportunity for learning and development. For the manager and the individual, it is difficult to predict whether the change will be perceived as positive or negative.

We are all creatures of habit and many of us want control over the pressures and stresses associated with work. We have preferred ways of doing things and prefer to seek changes rather than have them forced on us. When faced by sudden or unexpected change, people normally react in one of two ways:

- The change is regarded as threatening
- The change is regarded as an opportunity.

These two reactions describe opposite ends of a continuum, with many more subtly different reactions in between. You should be able to recognise different reactions in your team members when faced with change. Organisations and managers may consider that they have communicated the need for change well. They have communicated well in advance of the change, and have been honest, open and forthright. Often what they fail to do is to gauge the reactions of people. A key question to ask when communicating change to staff is: 'How do you feel about this?'

It is a question that needs to be asked several times as people's reactions to change vary and individual reactions also differ over time. Many people initially react to change negatively or suspiciously. It will take time for them to work through the options in their mind, sometimes after discussions with family, friends, their co-workers and manager. As the leader, you need to make time to show your staff where there are opportunities to be found in embracing the change. For example, there may be opportunities to raise the level of performance and, hence, reward and satisfaction.

Here is an example of how one organisation used a major change in strategy and operations as an opportunity to improve performance:

In 2000, BMW announced the sale of the UK Rover Car Group to another company, but that it was retaining the new Mini car (still in design stage) which would be built at the BMW plant in Cowley, Oxford, and distributed globally. Some people may have perceived the announcement as threatening – perhaps because they didn't want to work on a new model car, they didn't enjoy the idea of breaking away completely from the Rover way of operating, or they perceived that their jobs might be at risk because of the reorganisation. However, most of the Cowley staff perceived this information as an opportunity to remain in work, and be involved in a new and exciting project with large investment and long-term commitment to Cowley.

In a period of just over a year between 2000 and 2001, the following occurred at the BMW plant at Cowley:

- BMW sold most of the Rover group to a new company
- The Cowley site and many staff were retained to build the new Mini car
- Existing Rover car assembly lines at Cowley were dismantled and transported to the new Rover company in Birmingham
- New Mini assembly lines were designed and installed at Cowley

- The Cowley buildings were comprehensively overhauled – much of the work was undertaken by assembly-line workers, who would otherwise have been out of a job

- Assembly-line staff went on extended leave and some went to work at other BMW plants in Germany while the new lines were being built

- The new BMW culture began to permeate the plant

- Pre-production Minis received rave reviews from the motoring press in June 2001

- First sales to customers were scheduled for July 2001

- Staff and managers received extensive technical, personal, management and team development to help them cope with the new technology and new ways of working.

Development in a change environment

Development within a change environment is not very different from planned development. Both move people and organisations forward, and often the process is identical but the cycle time varies. Figure 4.2 shows the typical stages of the development process in organisations.

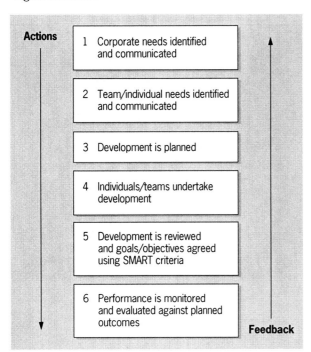

Figure 4.2 *Stages in development*

Change may mean that development takes priority over operations or production. A change, such as introducing new technology or processes, cannot occur until development has been undertaken.

The organisation will seek to plan for development but individuals always have responsibility for change.

Individual responsibility

Much of the responsibility for learning and development rests with individuals. This is especially so within a change environment. Many people sit back and say, 'If the company wants me to do something new or different, it's their responsibility to develop me.' Change is often complex and chaotic. Senior managers will be relying on a flexible, co-operative and proactive approach from all involved – managers and staff. What's more, although development planning may have been undertaken within the overall change plan, it is often the case that not all staff development needs are known from the outset. Sometimes development needs are identified only after changes have been implemented and their effects are better understood. In such circumstances, managers must seek to be in tune with what is happening in and around their areas of responsibility to keep pace with changes.

> There is no use whatever trying to help people who do not help themselves. You cannot push anyone up a ladder unless he be willing to climb himself.
>
> **Andrew Carnegie**
> **American industrialist**
> **(1835–1918)**

Activity 12
Change and development

Objective

This activity asks you to identify a change that is occurring, or which is planned, and chart the development needs associated with this change.

Task

1 Complete the chart by describing a change you are facing in your workplace.

The Change – Give a brief description:

Impact on people – What are the likely impacts of this change on the people involved?

How are you and the organisation geared to deal with these impacts, bearing in mind the range of individual reactions to change?

Benefits – List the benefits to the organisation and the people involved. Don't forget to list your suppliers and customers, as well as internal staff – if appropriate.

Organisation benefits   *People benefits*

Development needs – What staff development needs to be undertaken to enable the change to occur or to ensure its success? List in terms of outcomes.

Evaluation – How will you evaluate the success of the change and the development which contributed to it?

Evaluate the change   *Evaluate staff development*

2   If development is needed, discuss this with your manager and with staff.

Feedback

It is often easy to forget staff development needs in change events because a lot is occurring, much of which is new or different. People may be threatened by the changes occurring around them and over which they have little or no control. Your attention to their development needs may help to reassure them and should ensure they are capable of delivering what is needed.

Competencies

A competence is the ability to do a specific task to an acceptable level – to be competent. For example, to write a competent letter or to be a competent speaker. Competences may include skills, knowledge and attributes. A competency, on the other hand, is used in training and development to describe a set of knowledge, skills and behaviour that a jobholder needs to utilise in performing the job's tasks and responsibilities with competence.

Look at the following example of competencies at BMW.

BMW is one of the world's best-known brands. It manufactures and sells cars of high quality, most of which are the benchmark in various market segments. The BMW Leadership Model describes the range of behaviours which all managers must develop and demonstrate. While the description remains constant, BMW accepts that, being an international company, some flexibility is needed to cater for different cultural environments.

BMW Leadership Model

Personal performance: Leadership is about personal performance, contribution and risk taking, not just applying policies, procedures and systems

Realistic visions: Leaders inspire and motivate by creating and communicating realistic visions

Act as a role model, high standards: Leaders act as role models and earn respect through integrity and credibility. Leaders set high standards and apply such standards to themselves

To concentrate on achieving business goals: Leaders ensure the focus of attention is on achieving business goals and not on themselves

Objectives agreement/to encourage the willingness to change: Leaders establish agreed objectives and define the scope of their team members' autonomy and responsibility. They encourage and support initiative, creativity and willingness to change. Leaders revise objectives if conditions change

To communicate effectively/to build sound relationships: Leaders communicate effectively and build sound relationships

To create a working environment which stimulates enthusiasm and enjoyment: Leaders create a working environment which stimulates enthusiasm and enjoyment as well as focusing on business results

Confidence/consequences: Leaders build confidence through trust, if it is necessary they intervene decisively. They provide support and take on rather than evade responsibility for achieving the desired results

To achieve excellent team results: Leaders build efficient teams and actively develop all individuals. They encourage everyone to reach their full potential. True leaders do not hold people back

To operate effectively in different cultures: Leaders are able to operate effectively in different cultures and lead multicultural teams

Linking competencies to performance

Organisations may use competencies as part of their performance management system to align individual and team performance with the wider business goals and organisational strategy. See the example from Standard Chartered Bank below. The competency framework is a series of linked processes that includes identification of competencies, job descriptions, individual and team objectives, staff development, coaching and feedback. Its success in helping to promote high performance hinges on the active involvement and support of the manager.

Within the competency framework, the definitions are:

A **competency** – a set of knowledge, skills or behaviour needed in a business to ensure its success. Some competencies may be shared across all units in an organisation, but some may relate to job families or specific jobs, for example sales administration, project planning.

Core competencies – those competencies that apply across all units of an organisation, for example customer focus.

Competency level – the level at which a competency needs to be demonstrated to ensure success in a particular job.

Job competency profile – a summary of the different competencies and competency levels required for success in a particular job.

Personal competency profile – a summary of a person's level of attainment in each competency.

In Standard Chartered Bank, for example, a competency framework is used to identify the competencies at four different levels, where Level 4 relates to an entry-level job, typically junior staff who are task orientated, and Level 1 relates to an expert practitioner or business head with strategic responsibilities. The example below is taken from Standard Chartered's description of the core competency required of a change agent. The competency is divided into two areas:

♦ openness to change and innovation

♦ commitment.

This breakdown shows how the scope of responsibilities broadens from Level 4 through to Level 1.

Level 4	Level 3	Level 2	Level 1
Operates within established practices, accepting change and providing practical job-level feedback	Actively seeks improvements in day-to-day work and makes incremental changes within agreed parameters	Manages and implementation of change in own area of accountability	Leads business level change and complex reorganisation
Openness to change and innovation	*Openness to change and innovation*	*Openness to change and innovation*	*Openness to change and innovation*
Able to understand need for change and willingly accept it Able to identify workable ideas for improvement within own job	Able to look for ways of making improvements to existing services, work or operations Able to show a positive attitude to change and receptivity to new ideas	Able to contribute to the design of change at business level and to translate business level change initiatives into local action Able to encourage others in the business to implement creative solutions to problems	Able to display and communicate a vision for change for a large part of the Group Able to challenge the assumption of the Group and perceive complex, global problems and opportunities in new and innovative ways
Commitment-gaining	*Commitment-gaining*	*Commitment-gaining*	*Commitment-gaining*
Able to provide constructive feedback on the practical impact of changes in own job Able to demonstrate personal reliability through attention to detail and by putting in extra work as required	Able to provide constructive feedback about change processes in part of own business and to demonstrate commitment to change to other team members Understand that change involves personal risk and is able to treat own and others' well-intended errors as opportunities to learn	Able to gain commitment to new ideas and initiative which have an impact across the business area Able to convince others of the need to change and of their ability to contribute (through persuasion, empathy, modelling new behaviour, reward and recognition of key players etc.)	Understands and is able to address the issues involved in promoting major change in multinational organisations Able to enthuse people and lobby key influences across businesses and countries about the advantages of change, to build commitment and gain trust as the Group adopts new values and practices

Source: *Standard Chartered Bank* (used with permission)

Generic competencies

Some organisations apply generic competencies which are issued by lead industry or sector agencies, sponsored by government. For example, the Management Standards Centre (MSC) is the standards setting body for the National Occupational Standards for

Management. The management standards are available in vocational qualification format to enable individuals to work towards a nationally recognised qualification.

The management standards and qualifications apply at these levels of management:

1 Level 3 – junior managers/supervisors /team leaders.

2 Level 4 – middle managers.

3 Level 5 – senior managers.

The purpose, roles and examples of areas of competencies are described in detail.

In the US, the Department of Labor and Education formed the Secretary's Commission on Achieving Necessary Skills (SCANS) to study the kinds of competencies and skills that workers must have to succeed in today's workplace. The survey identified five key areas of competency:

♦ resources – identifies, plans and allocates resources

♦ interpersonal – works with others

♦ information – acquires and evaluates information

♦ systems – understands complex interrelationships

♦ technology – works with a variety of technologies.

Investors in People

Another source of support and guidance in the use of the competency framework is the government sponsored group called Investors in People (IIP). This is sometimes referred to as a model for determining an organisation's competencies for developing people. It is the UK national standard which sets the level of good practice for training and developing people to help organisations achieve their business goals. The standard was developed in 1990 in conjunction with the Confederation of British Industry, the Trades Union Congress and the Chartered Institute of Personnel and Development, and with the support of the Department of Employment.

The standards provide a national framework for improving business performance and competitiveness through a planned approach to communicating business objectives and developing people to meet these objectives.

There are 12 standards against which organisations can compare their current level of commitment and performance. These standards are based on four key principles:

- commitment to invest in people to achieve business goals
- planning how skills, individuals and teams are to be developed to achieve these goals
- taking action to develop and use necessary skills in a well-defined and continuing programme directly tied to business objectives
- evaluating outcomes of training and development for individuals' progress towards goals, the value achieved and future needs.

◆ Recap

This theme examines individual and team development in the context of a changing environment and the employee competencies required in the organisation.

Explore ways of finding development opportunities when tackling change

- As a manager your job is to help your team use change as an opportunity to learn and develop and, at the same time, to prevent them being overloaded with learning.

- Your role is to show your team members ways to embrace change and identify development needs in line with new objectives or changes in circumstances. Your focus on their needs will help to reassure individuals of their ability to cope with and benefit from, the change.

Identify how employee competencies can be linked to high performance

- Competencies set a standard for performance for which everyone needs to aim.

- Organisations may use competencies as part of their performance management system to align individual and team performance with the wider business goals and organisational strategy.

 **More @**

Thomson, R. (2002) 3rd edition, *Managing People*, Elsevier Butterworth-Heinemann

Managing People addresses the perspective of the individual manager whose role includes the management of people, as well as issues concerning the organisation as a whole. See particularly Chapter 11 'Managing in a changing world.'

Torrington, D. and Hall, L. (1998) 4th edition, *Human Resource Management*, FT Prentice Hall

This book is written from a practical management perspective. It explores change and human resource issues and provides a clear definition of competencies, showing how they can be used by organisations to help improve performance.

Investors in People – www.investorsinpeople.co.uk

For more information about the standards associated with the Investors in People awards, visit the group's website.

Management Standards Centre –
www.management-standards.org

For more information about management standards and competencies, visit this organisation's website.

Full references are provided at the end of the book.

Evaluating performance

Organisations are continually asking people to perform better. This theme examines ways to set and agree individual goals and provide objective feedback on performance. It also explores how to review team performance in a way that leads to performance improvements.

Is development working? There is more pressure today than ever before to produce results from staff development programmes and initiatives. If development is not shown to add value, it may be difficult to justify the expense. This theme looks at how monitoring, measurement and evaluation of development can be used as a management tool to determine what is and is not working as well as anticipated.

In this theme you will:

◆ **Explore the processes used to review individual and team performance**

◆ **Plan to meet the performance review needs of individuals**

◆ **Identify ways of evaluating development**

◆ **Consider ways of increasing the effectiveness of development.**

Performance reviews

A performance review or appraisal is where you provide feedback to your team and individual members of the team on their performance and set goals for the future. You should regard this as one of your most important responsibilities. The purpose of a performance review is to:

improve the individual's – and therefore, an organization's – performance. To do so, the appraisal has to be responsive to individual needs and be available to individuals throughout the organization.

Source: *Crainer* (1998)

Developing the performance review process

In developing a performance review process, an organisation must take into consideration:

- the organisation's goals and their link to individual needs

- the performance the organisation requires from the individual and the link to individual needs.

A framework for considering the performance review process is shown in Figure 5.1.

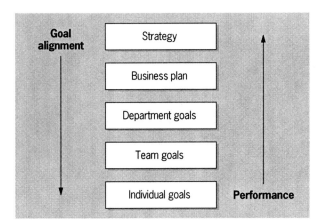

Figure 5.1 *Goal alignment for performance*

For performance reviews to have any value, organisations have to ensure that work is being organised efficiently and that the key processes are all aligned to ensure the production of goods or services that meet customers' needs.

Part of your responsibilities as a manager when organising work is to agree team and individual objectives. A review or appraisal is then conducted to match actual against targeted performance.

At an organisational level, the criteria for evaluating performance will range from shareholder value and stock market valuation, to profit margins at business and unit levels. There will of course be many other criteria applied, each of which will be used to ensure that the organisation is performing effectively.

At management level, the criteria include organisational performance measures, and performance measures for the individual and the team. The focus should be on the actual performance measure and also on how the performance was achieved. This gives an opportunity to link performance to development. Some features of the review would include:

- identifying factors that enhanced or hindered achievement

- any development that enhanced achievement

- personal commitment and contribution to the performance of the team

- approach taken to problem solving.

Why organisations undertake performance reviews

At a broad, strategic level, performance reviews indicate how well an organisation's workforce is performing against goals. If jobs are designed correctly and people are trained to undertake these jobs, then staff performance should fall within a normal distribution curve – see Figure 5.2.

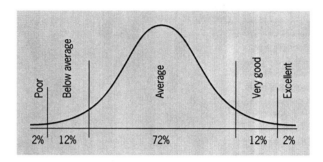

Figure 5.2 *Distribution of staff performance*

This normal distribution can be used at all levels in an organisation. Even in a department which contains many high fliers, the distribution should still be apparent, albeit that overall performance should be better than in others. Performance reviews assessed against the normal distribution curve help in spotting areas of underperformance. They also help in determining whether a manager is being too lenient or hard in assessing performance.

Mullins (1999) suggests several key benefits of a performance review process. It can:

♦ identify an individual's strengths and weaknesses, and indicate how strengths can be built upon and weaknesses overcome

♦ help to reveal problems that may be restricting progress and causing inefficiencies

♦ develop a greater degree of consistency through regular feedback on performance and discussions about potential

♦ provide information for staff planning, assist succession planning and determine suitability for promotion and particular types of employment

♦ improve communications by providing a forum for staff to talk about their ideas and expectations and how well they are progressing.

Types of review

There are two types of performance review:

◆ formal – which usually takes place at least once a year

◆ informal – ongoing, as and when appropriate.

We will look at each of these in turn.

Formal reviews

Most organisations undertake annual performance reviews, although some may undertake interim formal reviews at the six-month period and, under certain circumstances, more frequent formal reviews may take place, for example, for graduate trainees, high potential staff being considered for promotion, special appointments or for underperforming staff.

The performance review process
A typical performance review process may involve the following steps:

◆ Line manager receives forms from HR department

◆ Line manager distributes these to staff and asks them to review their own performance

◆ Staff complete forms and return them to manager

◆ Manager reviews individual performance and makes recommendations

◆ Manager conducts performance review interviews with individual members of staff

◆ Summary of meeting is recorded on the form which is signed by both parties and forwarded to senior manager or senior specialist for comment

◆ Senior manager may also record comments

◆ Form is returned to HR department, checked and, based on content, appropriate further actions are taken.

Organisations use a range of tools for assessing staff, and assessment may be against a number of criteria, such as achievement of objectives or achievement of competencies.

Annual performance reviews often carry an overall rating of performance and this rating may be used by organisations when determining an individual's pay rise or annual bonus. Organisations will already have the overall value of the pay rise or the size of the bonus pool in mind, and these may have been calculated against a normal distribution curve.

One side effect of directly linking performance reviews to pay is that the staff member involved in the review may tend to be less than frank about their own shortcomings if they fear a financial penalty is likely. A more objective outcome is likely if the performance review is divorced from the annual pay review.

James (1995) suggests that people work better when they are given:

- feedback on how they are performing
- clear attainable goals
- involvement in setting tasks and goals.

Informal reviews

People should not have to wait until an annual formal review to be told how they are doing. Feedback on performance should be regular and ongoing. Informal reviews include simple feedback, such as saying, 'That's great, well done...', that shows you are happy with the individual's overall performance. However, informal reviews also include occasional one-to-one meetings, where the manager and individual staff member consider any areas that are of concern.

Informal reviews are particularly useful in the following circumstances:

- when a person has done something praiseworthy
- when a person is new to the role or to the team
- when the role changes
- after the individual has attended a development event
- when the manager or team leader changes
- when objectives or targets are changed
- for the manager to make routine, regular checks on progress and to clarify any areas of concern
- for the manager to discuss performance before a coaching session
- to help determine the causes of good or poor performance.

Each of the above opportunities enables the manager to talk with an individual to explore areas of mutual interest and agree what is needed to help improve performance. It is an opportunity for both parties to voice any concerns, ask questions and clarify matters, explore options and agree how to proceed. Whenever appropriate, the manager should always reassure, praise and encourage the member of staff.

Informal performance reviews are often undertaken because an individual is underperforming. Rather than chastise the individual for poor performance, the manager should first use the review as an opportunity to identify the cause or causes. Often people do not perform well because of factors which may be unrelated to work, or because of factors which are outside their control. There may be family matters which are affecting an individual's concentration and performance, materials or information may arrive late, or equipment may be faulty. A quiet, friendly chat will reveal a lot more information than telling someone off before knowing all of the issues.

Conducting performance reviews

The way you conduct a formal review and an informal review meeting are broadly similar; it is the content of the review which differs. Your organisation may have some guidelines on how best to run reviews; you may find there are similarities with the following guidelines.

Guidelines for conducting reviews

Arrange a venue in which you know you will not be disturbed and agree the time and duration with the individual. It is important that you do not spring the meeting on a person – give prior notice. In some circumstances you may wish to reassure individuals that there is nothing for them to worry about – many people do worry about performance reviews, especially informal reviews unless they are a common feature.

During the meeting:

- State the reason for the meeting and the agenda – what you want both parties to get out of it – and the time you have set aside for the meeting.

- Open the review by asking the individual how they believe they are performing or how they are getting on. A good starting point is to ask them to talk you through their self-assessment form, if they have completed one. Ask questions to clarify and widen your knowledge and understanding of the topics under review.

- Respond with the facts and your observations and views, but do not get involved in a debate. Debates may get heated and are not conducive to a constructive dialogue. The very nature of performance reviews is that they should be a mixture of fact and opinion. As the manager, you have a duty to ensure that your opinion is well informed, and based on first-hand and accurate observations and evidence. The facts should speak for themselves. If people do not initially accept your views and try to engage you in a debate, ask them to reflect on the matters under discussion and perhaps offer them the opportunity for a further meeting.

- Start with an overview of the goals which were agreed or set and then undertake a structured review of each, mentioning any specific factors which may have hindered or enhanced

99

performance. It is important that you discuss the issues and not the personality behind the issues.

◆ Be specific, especially if you are discussing areas of underperformance. You should be able to state clearly what did or did not occur and when, and the impact it had on performance. You may wish to refer to standards, measurements, statistics and specific occurrences that support your views. Examine causes, what went well, why and how. Consider a few important issues in order to keep the review manageable and to avoid overwhelming an individual with too much detailed feedback.

◆ Ask the individual how they plan to improve. Agree how changes or improvements can be implemented, and what other help, coaching and assistance may be given. Initiate a dialogue on future actions and goals, and how they will be achieved.

◆ Confirm how you will monitor progress and the ongoing feedback you wish to gain from the individual on their work.

◆ Review the agenda to ensure you have covered all issues.

◆ Try to end on a positive, encouraging note, close on time and make a written record of the discussion and actions agreed.

After the meeting, monitor performance and find opportunities to continue to provide feedback on a few important issues.

Kathy Gagne (2001) suggests the following four key points when reviewing staff performance:

Give honest feedback – don't try to protect underperforming staff because of fear of confrontation.

Ask questions – encourage people to reflect on their own performance and their understanding of their job and responsibilities.

Focus on the future – establish the objectives for the next period, and the development and support needed to meet them.

Communicate organisational goals – use the review to keep people informed of shifts in the organisation's priorities.

Keeping notes on performance

It is good practice for team leaders and managers to make informal, ongoing notes about people and their performance. This is a very useful process because it is impossible to remember every aspect of an individual's performance throughout the period under review.

Regular note taking of both facts and opinions is an excellent counter against staff who make a determined effort to perform better in the period immediately prior to formal reviews in the belief that their managers have short memories.

If you make regular notes, remember to keep them in a safe place and don't commit anything to print that you are not prepared to discuss openly. Bear in mind that the Data Protection Act 1998 affords people the right to access records about themselves.

The Data Protection Act 1998, which covers both the public and the private sector throughout the United Kingdom, gives individuals a right to find out what information, including personnel information, is held about them on computer and in some manual records.* This is known as the right of subject access. There is also a right to have inaccurate data corrected, blocked, erased or destroyed, and to seek compensation through the courts for damage and distress caused by such inaccuracy or by any other contravention of the Act.

* The Act applies to records held in manual filing systems if these are structured by reference to individuals or by criteria relating to individuals, and allow easy access to the personal data they contain.

Source: *Data Protection Act 1998*

Activity 13

Performance review in your organisation

Objective

This activity asks you to identify your organisation's current approach to performance reviews, and to compare this with a suggested generic process for performance review.

Task

1 Compare your organisation's performance review process with the process outlined here. How does it differ? Make comments alongside your ticks or crosses.

Generic performance review process	What happens in your organisation ✓ or ✗
Line manager receives forms from HR with notes for guidance on completing	☐
Distributes forms and notes to staff, asks them to review their own performance	☐
Staff complete forms and return to manager	☐
Manager agrees a time and date, books a room and conducts individual performance review discussions	☐
Summary of each discussion is recorded on forms and both parties sign	☐
Forms are forwarded to senior manager or senior specialist (second reports) who may just sign as agreeing original comments or may add further comments	☐
If the second reports show significantly different comments, forms are returned to manager and individuals are notified. Forms may be re-signed by individuals	☐
Forms contain overall performance scores against a known scale	☐
Overall performance score may be used to help identify:	
◆ career advancement or other job opportunities	☐
◆ long-term development	☐
◆ succession planning	☐
◆ individual/team bonuses or rewards	☐
◆ individual objectives	☐

2 From your comments, how effective is your organisation's performance review process? You may feel that your organisation's established process works extremely well.

Comment on your organisation's performance review process:

3 What improvements, if any, would you recommend to your organisation's process? Can you suggest improvements to make it better for your staff?

Ideas for improvement:

Feedback

An effective performance review process ensures that effort is aligned with strategy. You have a key role to play in ensuring this link is made and enhanced, but the link should be made in conjunction with each member of your team. You should also bear in mind the problems often associated with linking performance review with assessment for reward, as concerns about reward can undermine efforts to focus on performance. For people to be fully committed to work, they should contribute to and agree their objectives or goals – thereby ensuring their buy-in.

Activity 14
Carrying out informal performance reviews

Objective

Use this activity to reflect on your informal performance review feedback process, and to plan to get to know the review needs of your team members.

Task

1   Reflect on how you give informal reviews by answering the following questions. You may like to write on a separate sheet of paper.

When was the last time you had an informal review with each team member?

What topics were discussed?

What outcomes/ongoing actions were agreed?

What monitoring, measurement and evaluation of each individual's performance have you conducted?

Have you made notes or are you relying on memory?

Do you have specific information about the individual's performance which you can refer to when discussing aspects of good/average/poor performance with people – as well as your general view?

What is it that you will discuss with individuals in each informal review?

What are the key thoughts/messages you wish to get across?

2 How aware are you of what your team members require from you in terms of informal reviews?

Plan to speak to each member of your team to ascertain the nature and level of feedback each of them would like to receive from you.

Feedback

Demonstrating your sensitivity and flexibility in meeting people's different needs will enhance your individual and team relationships. However, you should remember that all feedback needs to be accurate, clear and appropriate and, in some cases, timely. On the subject of time, you will need to ensure that you give sufficient time to meet people's informal performance review needs.

Monitoring and evaluating development

Some organisations pay great attention to the monitoring, measurement and evaluation of staff development. Some organisations state that they intuitively know whether development is working, without the need to implement time-consuming monitoring, measuring and evaluation processes. In some respects, development becomes an act of faith.

> A major international bank sends high-flying middle managers to one of the world's top business schools for a three-week strategic banking programme. The overall cost of this programme, including lost opportunity, airfares and accommodation, is very expensive. The programme and its outputs are not monitored, measured or evaluated, but the business unit heads have high regard for the programme and so continue to make provision for it in their business development budgets.

One of the main reasons that organisations do not always evaluate the return on their development investment is that they contend that it is difficult or impossible to separate out the development event from other factors involved in changes in performance or outputs. If it isn't measurable, it isn't seen as a priority. The counter view is that, although difficult, the effects of development can be measured through appropriate evaluation techniques.

Establishing a focus on outputs

For many years, line and development managers have asked the question: 'What are the objectives for this development programme or event?' It is only relatively recently that more widespread questions have been asked about outputs. Now managers are asking: 'What are the work-based outputs I wish to achieve?' or 'What needs to happen in the workplace and what development will make or help it happen?' If managers are clear about the outputs they want to achieve, it is possible to ensure a close fit with the development process that is needed.

Linking development and evaluation

Figure 5.3 shows how a development process should look if all components are in place.

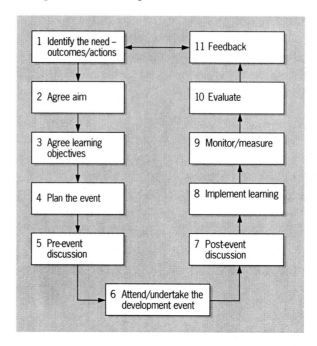

Figure 5.3 *Development and evaluation*

We will look at each of these in turn.

Identify the need. Development needs are identified either from top down or bottom up and should be aligned with the organisation's goals. In some cases, this may be more of an act of faith, because certain aspects of personal and management development are often less tangible than technical or job-related development. The judgement of the manager is important in determining or confirming specific needs.

Outcomes. These are the results that the department or unit wishes to achieve in the workplace from its investment in the development event. Good questions to ask are: 'What is it that needs to happen in the workplace?' or 'What added value will accrue to the department if people undertake this development?'

Aim. This is a broad description of the learning event. It can be simply a sentence or short paragraph. For example, 'The aim of this programme is to introduce managers to a range of motivational theories and techniques, which they may apply in conjunction with their team leadership responsibilities'.

Objectives. These cover the scope of learning in the development event. They may also cover the learning methodology. In some cases, objectives may include both primary and secondary considerations. For example, a programme may be designed primarily to 'improve problem solving and decision making', but secondary objectives may be 'to enhance communication skills, teamworking and networking'.

Planning. There are two separate aspects of planning:

- The event has to be planned, which involves design, resources, facilities, venue, budget
- The manager has to organise the people involved in the development, which includes planning for their absences from work.

Pre-event discussion. This is an opportunity for the manager to reaffirm the rationale for the individual who is undertaking the development. Managers often state their expectations and provide pointers towards specific aspects of the event, linking it to the individual's development and the business need.

Undertaking development. There are many forms of development, suffice to say that the success of a development event, whether it is attending a residential course, reading a book or secondment to another department, is reliant upon the commitment of the individual.

Post-event discussion. This is, arguably, the most important discussion a manager will have with staff attending a development event. It is important to know if they enjoyed the event. If a person has enjoyed a learning experience, they will remember more of it for a longer period of time and be more disposed to apply the learning in the workplace.

Implement learning. The manager has an important role in providing opportunities for staff to apply what they have learned in the workplace. The manager may act as a coach in this or may simply provide informal, ad-hoc support.

Monitor and measure. The form of monitoring that a manager employs following staff development varies widely according to the situation. However, monitoring normally comprises a mixture of first-hand observations and feedback from other team members and the individual's suppliers and customers. Monitoring may also require the individual to make regular reports to the manager.

Measurement and monitoring are often interlinked. Some managers may say that intangible development is difficult or impossible to measure, for example we cannot measure morale. However, we can measure the factors which impact on good or poor morale. Measurement criteria should be agreed at the post-event discussion and regular checks or reports should be made to ensure work is on track.

Evaluation. Common reasons for evaluating development include:

- to validate development as a business tool aimed at profitability
- to justify the costs incurred
- to help improve the design of events
- to help in selecting development methods.

The Kirkpatrick model of evaluation

There are several well-known and commonly used models for measuring the effectiveness of development. One way of undertaking a structured review process is to apply the Kirkpatrick model which examines development at four levels, as shown in Table 5.1. This model was first published in 1983 and is widely used throughout the UK.

---

1 Reaction

Were participants pleased with the programme or learning event?

Did the event deliver what was promised?

This is normally undertaken by a survey at the end of, or immediately following a programme. It is of limited value, but an individual's overall and immediate feelings about an event can have a bearing on their willingness to implement the learning in the workplace. One of the best uses of a reactive survey is to determine participants' views on:

- *location/facilities*
- *event structure/pace*
- *pace and depth, and breadth of content*
- *compatibility with individual learning styles*
- *applicability to them/their job*
- *tutor approach/capability*
- *time given to individual coaching*
- *the action plan they intend to implement.*

2 Learning

What did participants learn?

Can they apply the knowledge or skills acquired?

This can be assessed by tests during or after the development event. Some tests confirm short-term recall only, others confirm aptitude and skills capability. The imposition of tests usually means that some people will concentrate harder than otherwise – meaning they should learn more.

3 Behaviour

What the learning transferred back to the workplace.

Did behaviours change based on what was learned?

This is assessed by monitoring in the workplace. Changes in behaviours are very dependent on the syllabus and individual reactions to the learning. To monitor changes in behaviours, managers must first have a good understanding of previous behaviour and of the new standards they expect.

4 Results

Did the changes in behaviour or the skills learned positively affect the organisation?

What was the impact on the bottom line?

This is assessed by monitoring in the workplace and measuring results against goals or objectives. Agreeing objectives using the SMART criteria plays an important part in measuring added value results.

Table 5.1 *The Kirkpatrick evaluation model*

Source: *Adapted from Kirkpatrick (1983)*

The difficulty with evaluating the effectiveness of development is that it takes time and it may not be the only factor which has contributed to changes in performance. Like many other processes within an organisation, if the right criteria are included at the input stage, it is easier to measure and evaluate the outputs later on.

Activity 15
Evaluating development in your organisation

Objective

Use this final activity to compare your organisation's evaluation of development with the Kirkpatrick model.

Task

1 The chart gives a series of questions for each of the four levels in Kirkpatrick's model of evaluation to identify current evaluation practices in your organisation.

Kirkpatrick's model	Questions to ask of your organisation
Reaction	Do you meet with all participants to gain their first-hand comments?
	Did participants complete a questionnaire at the end of the event?
	Who designed the questionnaire – you, development staff or the supplier of the development event?
	Whose needs does the questionnaire meet?
	Do you see copies of these questionnaires, or do they go to the training and development department?
	What do these questionnaires actually tell you?
	How do you rate your organisation's processes in this area?

Kirkpatrick's model	Questions to ask of your organisation
Learning	Can you make clear connections between the programme objectives, the learning gained and the desired outcomes?
	What processes does your organisation typically employ to measure learning gained?
	Who determines/designs/monitors/evaluates these measurement processes, and for what purposes are they used?
	How do you rate your organisation's processes in this area?
Behaviour	What processes are currently adopted by your organisation to measure behavioural changes following development events?
	How do you currently measure behavioural changes in individuals following development events?
	How do you rate the effectiveness of these processes?
	How do you rate your organisation's processes in this area?
Results	What processes does your organisation currently operate to determine the results of development investment?
	Do you undertake post-event discussions with your staff?
	Do you agree new/changed goals/targets/objectives which include measurable (SMART) criteria?
	Do you monitor performance or observe behaviours which impact on outputs?
	Do you compare actual outputs achieved against desired outputs (those outputs which were first agreed and which led to the development event)?
	Do you evaluate the hard and soft data gathered?
	Can you clearly state whether each development event attended by your staff has made a difference, the nature of the difference and the impact on organisational performance?
	What data do you have to substantiate your views?
	Do you currently provide feedback to individuals on the nature of their improved (or otherwise) performance following participation in a development event?
	How do you rate your organisation's processes in this area?

Feedback

You may wish to discuss current evaluation practices in your organisation with colleagues, your manager or training and development staff. What improvements do you think could be made? If your organisation fails to measure the effectiveness of development, do you think there is a danger that the organisation will fail to value development?

◆ Recap

This theme explores the processes used to evaluate performance.

Explore the processes used to review individual and team performance

- There are two types of performance review – formal and informal. The formal review is likely to include feedback on how individuals and teams are performing, setting clear, attainable goals and a dialogue to agree goals and tasks.

- Informal reviews are likely to be more ad hoc and based on good or poor performance, changes in leadership, targets or objectives or for regular monitoring of performance.

- The key points in reviewing staff performance are:
  - Give honest feedback
  - Ask questions
  - Focus on the future
  - Communicate organisational goals.

Plan to meet the performance review needs of individuals

- To meet the performance review needs of individuals you need to review the processes you use to carry out formal performance reviews

- Use informal performance reviews to keep up to date with individual development. By demonstrating your flexibility and sensitivity to the needs of others you will enhance team relationships.

Identify ways of evaluating development

- Asking questions such as, 'What are the work-based outputs we wish to achieve?' and 'What development will make it happen?' will enable managers to ensure a close fit with the development process.

- The Kirkpatrick model is a structured evaluation tool for considering the effectiveness of development. It is based on four levels of review: reaction, learning, behaviour and results.

Consider ways of increasing the effectiveness of development

- The activity on evaluating development in your organisation provides some useful guidance on ways to increase the effectiveness of development interventions.

- Setting clear goals and objectives for development will help you to measure its success and effectiveness. By making clear connections with workplace practice and organisational objectives you will increase the effectiveness and value of the development activities.

 More @

Phillips, J. J. (1997) *Handbook of Training Evaluation and Measurement Methods*, Gulf Publishing
This book illustrates how to design, implement and assess the effectiveness of human resource development (HRD) programmes, and how to measure their return on investment (ROI).

Thomson, R. (2002) 3rd edition, *Managing People*, Elsevier Butterworth-Heinemann
Managing People addresses the perspective of the individual manager whose role includes the management of people, as well as issues concerning the organisation as a whole. See Chapter 8 'Managing performance' and in particular the sections 'Training and developing your staff', 'Methods of development' and 'Staff development outside the organisation'.

Torrington, D. and Hall, L. (1998) 4th edition, *Human Resource Management*, Prentice Hall Europe
This book is written from a practical management perspective. It explores various methods of evaluating training.

Tyson, S. and York, A. (2000) 4th edition, *Essentials of HRM*, Elsevier Butterworth-Heinemann
Essentials of HRM combines an overview of organisational behaviour with a detailed explanation of human resources management policies and techniques. It also acts as an introduction to the study of industrial relations. See Part 4 on training and development and assessing performance.

References

Antonioni, D. (2000) 'Leading, Managing and Coaching', *Industrial Management*, September

Bilmes, L. (2001) 'Scoring goals for people and company', *Financial Times*, 26 November

Caldwell, B. J. and Carter, E. (eds) (1993) *The Return of the Mentor: Strategies for Workplace Learning*, Falmer Press

Cates, K. and Rahimi, K. (2001) 'Algebra lessons for older workers', in a survey in *Mastering Management* series in *Financial Times*, 19 November

Conger, J. (1998) 'How Gen X managers manage', *Strategy and Business*, First Quarter

Coupland, D. (1996) *Generation X*, Abacus

Crainer, S. (1998) 3rd edition, *Key Management Ideas*, Financial Times Pitman Publishing

Data Protection Act 1998, The Stationery Office Ltd, www.hmso.gov.uk/acts/acts1998/19980029.htm

Drucker, P. (1974) *Management: Tasks, Responsibilities, Practices*, Elsevier Butterworth-Heinemann

Gagne, K. (2001) 'Your performance review: make it perform', *Business Week*, 17 December

Harvey-Jones, J. (1990) *Making It Happen*, Fontana

Hersey, P. (1984) *The Situational Leader*, Leadership Studies inc

Hersey, P. and Blanchard, K. H. (1993) 6th edition, *Management of Organizational Behavior: Utilizing Human Resources*, FT Prentice Hall

Holmes, K. (1999) *Interviews and Appraisals*, Orion Business Books

Honey, P. and Mumford, A. (1982) *The Manual of Learning Styles*, Peter Honey, 10 Linden Avenue, Maidenhead, Berks

Investors in People, www.investorsinpeople.co.uk

James, G. (1995) 'Performance Appraisal', *Administrator*, June

Jennings, D. and Wattam, S. (1998) 2nd edition, *Decision Making: An Integrated Approach*, FT Pitman Publishing

Johnson, L. J. (2001) 'Coaching and Mentoring', *Manage*, May

Kanter, R. M. (1988) 4th impression, *The Change Masters*, Routledge

Kirkpatrick, D. L. (1983) 'Four Stages to Measuring Training Effectiveness', *Personnel Administrator*, November

Kolb, D. (1985) *Experiential Learning: Experience as the Source of Learning and Development*, FT Prentice Hall

Lambert, T. (1996) *Key Management Solutions*, FT Pitman Publishing

Management Standards Centre, www.managementstandards.org

Minter, R. L. and Thomas, E. G. (2000) 'Employee development through coaching, mentoring and counselling: a multidimensional approach,' *Review of Business*, Summer, p.45

Mullins, L. J. (1999) 5th edition, *Management and Organisational Behaviour*, FT Pitman Publishing

Parsloe, E. (1992) *Coaching, Mentoring and Assessing*, Kogan Page

Peters, T. and Waterman, R. (1982) *In Search of Excellence*, HarperCollins

Revans, R. W. (1982) *The ABC of Action Learning*, Chartwell Bratt

Revans, R. (1996) in an interview by Stuart Crainer in the *Mastering Management* series in *Financial Times*, 12 April

Secretary's Commission on Achieving Necessary Skills, www.doleta.gov/SCANS

Tannenbaum, R. and Schmidt, W. H. (1973) 'How to choose a leadership pattern', *Harvard Business Review*, May/June

Thomson, R. (1998) *People Management*, Orion Business Books

Torrington, D. and Hall, L. (1998) 4th edition, *Human Resource Management*, FT Prentice Hall Europe

Urwick, L. (1952) quoted in Mullins, L. (1999) 5th edition, *Management and Organisational Behaviour*, FT Prentice Hall